JOYCE H. SEXTON

The Slandered Woman in Shakespeare

ELS

EDITIONS

ELS Editions
Department of English
University of Victoria
Victoria, BC
Canada V8W 3W1
www.elseditions.com

Founding Editor: Samuel L. Macey

General Editor: Luke Carson

Printed by CreateSpace

English literary studies monograph series
ISSN 0829-7681 ; 12
ISBN-10 0-920604-22-6
ISBN-13 978-0-920604-22-9

TO MY MOTHER AND FATHER

CONTENTS

ACKNOWLEDGEMENTS

I owe the most to Professor Madeleine Doran, who got me started on this project and helped me with her criticism, "sharper than the sword" but always gracious; and Professor Standish Henning, who read several drafts and gave advice that always worked. I am also indebted to the National Endowment for the Humanities for a stipend some summers ago, and to Professor Ray Heffner for a helpful review along the way. I thank my husband as much for his healthful skepticism as for his support; my children, Ann and Elizabeth, for their adaptability; and, for various contributions to my older daughter's life during my working hours, the Children's Television Workshop, Miss Betty's Pre-School, and Christian Caulum.

A previous version of this study was written as a University of Wisconsin doctoral dissertation (1966). The chapter on *Much Ado* was printed in slightly different form in *Philological Quarterly*, LIV (1975), 419-33.

PREFACE

Shakespeare's four plays on the theme of the slandered woman have not previously been discussed as a group. By examining them together, I hoped in this study to show how they illuminate one another. Remarkably similar in basic design, *Much Ado, Othello, Cymbeline,* and *The Winter's Tale* reveal Shakespeare's lasting absorption with the theme of false accusation. The lack of psychological realism in these plays has long been acknowledged; but we have not recognized that in them Shakespeare was deliberately, specifically, and consistently sacrificing realism in order to emphasize this theme. These plays (their composition spanning the last half of his career as a dramatist) are a window on Shakespeare's evolving imagination. I have not intended to offer comprehensive critical analyses of them but instead to point out the centrality of the theme common to them all and to outline the aesthetic choices which Shakespeare made in order to achieve this emphasis. Especially in the case of *Othello* it is obvious that I have seemed to isolate an actually inseparable part from a whole in order to view my subject clearly.

CHAPTER ONE

"Slander's Venom'd Spear":[1] The Tradition

About mid-way through his career as a dramatist, in 1598 or 1599, Shakespeare took up the theme of the slandered woman. From a familiar story (one he could have found in Ariosto, Bandello, and Spenser, among others) of a bride falsely accused by a rejected suitor, he created the main plot of *Much Ado about Nothing*. But Hero, Claudio, and Don John, as it turned out, were just a beginning. In some five years Shakespeare returned to the theme, this time transmuting a "true" tale (from Cinthio's *Hecatommithi*) of disappointed passion, vengeful slander, and violent murder—a simple, crude narrative—into great tragedy: *Othello*. Then, after another five years approximately, now near the end of his writing career, he took over a story from the *Decameron* in which the villain calumniates a woman so that he may appear to have won a wager; this became *Cymbeline*. The next romance, *The Winter's Tale*, was Shakespeare's final portrayal of the slandered heroine.

The plays form a remarkable set—unique, in fact, in Shakespeare. This is the only type-story that he used as the main plot of four different plays. We may wonder what particularly there was in it that appealed to him again and again. We are enlightened by both the resemblances and the differences among the plays. The stories of Hero, Desdemona, Imogen, and Hermione are similar structurally: four tracings of one basic pattern. Shakespeare rearranged quite consistently the various materials—in continental epic and novel, English allegory and romance—which make up the long list of sources for these works. Whatever the aesthetic rationale or the ethical intent of a given predecessor, Shakespeare designed each play so as to emphasize the strong lines inherent in the story and to insist on a particular conception: that good name has absolute value, that (as Mowbray puts it to King Richard):

> The purest treasure mortal times afford
> Is spotless reputation: that away,
> Men are but gilded loam or painted clay.
> A jewel in a ten-times-barr'd-up chest
> Is a bold spirit in a loyal breast.

11

> Mine honour is my life; both grow in one;
> Take honour from me, and my life is done.[2]

In contrast to their sources for the most part, *Much Ado, Othello, Cymbeline*, and *The Winter's Tale* concentrate on the idea that slander, the enemy of honor, is a peculiarly powerful and destructive force in society. It was a theme worthy of repetition.

As variations on a theme the four plays illuminate one corner of Shakespeare's imagination. They differ sharply not only in kind and mood but in degree of emphasis on motive, act, consequence. As slander stories *Much Ado* and *Othello* reveal the author's interest in motivation especially. In the sources of *Much Ado*, the slanderer had been impelled by revenge: rejected love turned to hate. Shakespeare changed the villain profoundly. He discarded the received motive and suggested another, one less readily intelligible but interesting enough to be re-examined in another play. Don John is a sketch of the envious man, who needs no real motivation beyond his own spite; and Iago (whose prototype in the source is also a rejected suitor) is the finished portrait, although he is also much more. Having created Iago, made envy and slander so real in this character that he defies final analysis, Shakespeare turned in *Cymbeline* and *The Winter's Tale* to the other side of the story. Iachimo's motivation, a mixture, is not very important; Leontes has no motive at all (his jealousy, his opinion that his wife has betrayed him, being a "disease"). In the romances what absorbs us most is the meaning of reputation as the "purest treasure mortal times afford," the evil of words which strike at reputation, however they may be prompted. These plays, until their miraculous conclusions, are spectacles of loss and pain brought about by the instrument "Whose edge is sharper than the sword. . . . "[3] But whether focussing on motive or deed, Shakespeare was always exploiting the underlying theme in his slander plays.

This theme was a very old one, and its expression had long before Shakespeare's age become conventionalized. Sixteenth-century artists inherited directly from the Middle Ages (primarily through the tradition of the Seven Deadly Sins)[4] a precise definition of slander, a vocabulary through which it was customarily expressed, and a set of associated ideas and images. In the Sins tradition slander, or detraction, was usually thought of as a form, method, or product of the most devilish Sin, the "werst of alle synnes": Envy.[5] Writers like Gower, Chaucer, and Lydgate, whose extended allegories on the Sins formed part of the imaginative inheritance of sixteenth-century artists, presented detraction as essentially envious. Their literary treatments of the Sins, alongside a continuing homiletic tradition, helped to perpetuate through Shakespeare's lifetime the sense that slander is peculiarly devilish, in effect even when not in inception. And this idea is fundamental to Shakespeare's plays on the subject.

The medieval tradition had its roots in yet older formulations: classical, scriptural, patristic. If we look at some of the earlier representations of envy and slander and then review the definitions of these sins in medieval literature, we shall have a background against which to view sixteenth-century images; Shakespeare's contemporaries, especially Spenser, testify to the unfaded vitality of the ancient theme. Within this framework Shakespeare's treatments will become more clearly intelligible.

The Classics; the Church Fathers; the Late Medieval Tradition

From classical ethical speculation and classical poetry come an enduring characterization of envy, defined by Aristotle as "pain at the sight of [others'] good fortune."[6] Ovid's personification of *Invidia*, the *locus classicus*, is to become engraved upon the European imagination. In *Metamorphoses* II Minerva, cherishing a grudge against an Athenian girl, seeks out Envy's dark cave; within is "Envy, eating snakes' flesh, the proper food of her venom. . . . Pallor o'erspreads her face and her whole body seems to shrivel up. Her eyes are all awry, her teeth are foul with mould; green, poisonous gall o'erflows her breast, and venom drips down from her tongue. She never smiles, save at the sight of another's troubles; she never sleeps, being filled with wakeful cares; unwelcome to her is the sight of men's success and with the sight she pines away; she gnaws and is gnawed, herself her own punishment."[7] No visualization of envy is ever to be more influential; this face and figure will be sketched repeatedly by Church Fathers, medieval preachers, sixteenth century bishops. Innumerable artists through Shakespeare's time will re-create the pallor and skew eyes; the teeth livid with film, filth, rust, blight, or mildew (*livent robigine dentes*); the leanness (*macies*) and wakefulness, pining (*intabesco*) and gnawing (*carpo*). Ovid's Envy, ordered by Minerva to "infect" the Athenian girl with spiteful grief over her sister's approaching marriage to Mercury, travels with a staff made of thorns (*spineus*): "Wherever she goes, she tramples down the flowers, causes the grass to wither, blasts the high waving trees, and taints with the foul pollution of her breath whole peoples, cities, homes" (791-94). When she fills her victim with "pestilential, poisonous breath" (800), the girl quickly becomes an image of Envy herself. Groaning and pining away because another is happy, she is consumed "just as when a fire is set under a pile of weeds,

13

which give out no flames and waste away with slow consumption" (810-11). As punishment for her attempt to thwart the marriage, Mercury turns her to stone. "And, as an incurable cancer spreads its evil roots ever more widely and involves sound with infected parts," so does a deadly chill stop her vital functions (825-28). All of this—the poison and pollution, the fire, consumption and cancer—will be utterly commonplace in future discussions of envy.[8] Elsewhere in the literature of antiquity *Invidia* is endowed with sharp teeth and pointed weapons: "all glory is shattered by Envy's nigh-awaiting dart," writes Virgil,[9] and Horace rejoices that "Envy, in spite of herself, will ever admit that I have lived with the great, and, while trying to strike her tooth on something soft, will dash upon what is solid."[10] Plutarch uses another kind of image, equally enduring: " . . . just as beetles appear most of all in grain when it is ripe for harvest and in roses when they are in full bloom, so envy fastens most of all on characters and persons that are good and increasing in virtue and fame."[11] And envy, conventionally associated with slander, is the enemy of fame. Ovid is thankful that his Muse has given him "a lofty name —the name which renown is wont to give only after death. Nor has jealousy [*livor*], that detractor of the present, attacked with malignant teeth any work of mine."[12] Cicero defends an envied man, a victim of slander's tooth.[13] Horace warns us against "malice, seeing that we live in that kind of a world where keen envy and slander are so rife."[14] Terence writes, "invidere omnes mihi, / mordere clanculum" (Everybody envies me and backbites me).[15] Slander is the speech of envy: "livida lingua."[16]

The Church Fathers' discussions of envy blend the ancients' ideas, language, and imagery with Biblical dicta and Christian theology. Treatises by Saint Cyprian, third-century bishop of Carthage, and Basil the Great (fourth century), give us a glimpse of the Deadly Sin as it begins to develop. The Fathers present the Scriptural interpretation of invidiousness: "For God created man incorruptible . . . / But through envy of the Devil came death into the world; and they follow him that are of his side."[17] "What drove the Devil, that author of evils, to wage furious war upon mankind?" asks Basil. "Was it not envy?"[18] And the war goes on: with envy as his only weapon "the Devil, the destroyer of our life, has been inflicting wounds upon all men and striking them down from the foundation of the world, and he will continue to do so until its consummation" (Basil, p. 468).

Cyprian, quoting from the First Epistle of John (2.11), identifies enviousness with hatred: "He who hates his brother walks in the darkness and does not know where he goes."[19] A gratuitous quality is suggested: "It is a persevering evil to persecute a man who belongs to the grace of God; it is a calamity without a remedy to hate one who is happy" (Cyprian, p. 300).

Cain, Esau, and Saul exemplify "envy and murder, crimes of brother against brother" (Basil, p. 465). And it was "that very bitter envy ... which the madness of the Jews caused to break out against the Saviour" (Basil, p. 468).

A psychological portrait of the invidious man, combining classical and Christian features, emerges. While every other sin is "brought to an end by its consummation," this one is a "continually abiding evil and a sin without end" (Cyprian, pp. 298-99), insatiable like Satan's spite. This emotion gives rise to hatred, animosity, avarice, ambition, pride, cruelty, faithlessness, impatience, discord, and anger: it is the "root of all evils" (Cyprian, pp. 297-98). The envier disguises his feelings: "ashamed to make known his sad condition," he "confines in the depths of his soul this disease which is gnawing at his vitals and consuming them" (Basil, p. 464). This, above all other vices, "causes double-dealing among men. Hypocrites maintain an outward semblance of charity, while keeping their hatred deeply hidden within, like rocks under the surface of the sea, which, being covered with shallow water, bring unforeseen disaster to the unwary" (Basil, p. 474).[20] There is a natural affinity between envy and slander: "Envious persons are skilled in making what is praiseworthy seem despicable by means of unflattering distortions and in slandering virtue through the vice that is neighbor to it" (Basil, p. 471). Paul characterized the speech of the envious: "The venom of asps is under their lips: and their mouth is full of cursing and bitterness" (Cyprian, p. 299).[21]

The theologians' imagery recalls the Roman poets, the Psalmist, the Apostle. Cyprian uses Ovidian diction: envy is the gnawing worm of the soul (*anima tinea*), the pestilence or rotting of thoughts (*cogitationum tabes*), a rust of the heart (*pectoris rubigo*). With the invidious there is always sighing and groaning, and the fire burns ever more hotly (pp. 298-99). Here, in derived language, Cyprian exhorts the envier to abandon his malice: "Tear out of your heart the thorns and thistles [*spinas et tribulos*]. Expel the venom of gall [*venena fellis*]; cast out the virus of discords; let the mind which the jealousy of the serpent had infected be cleansed; let all the bitterness which had settled within be softened by the sweetness of Christ" (p. 307). The Fathers compare envy to the serpent, the swift arrow. Envy "consumes the soul that gives it birth, like the vipers which are said to be born by eating their way through the womb that conceived them" (Basil, p. 463). And: "As arrows shot with great force come back upon the archer when they strike a hard and unyielding surface, so also do the movements of envy strike the envious person himself and they harm the object of his spite not at all" (Basil, p. 469). Basil likens envy, the "plague of friendship," to the red blight, the "common pest to corn" (p. 460). And he uses a simile which will captivate many other analysts of this moral failing: "As vultures are attracted to ill-

15

smelling places and fly past meadow after meadow and pleasant, fragrant regions, as flies pass by healthy flesh and swarm eagerly to a wound, so the envious avert their gaze from the brightness in life and the loftiness of good actions and fix their attention upon rottenness" (Basil, p. 470). Later the canker may be substituted for the worm, or the nettle for the thistle; the vulture becomes the hyena, hoopoe, or dung beetle; but these comparisons, like most of the figures the Fathers employ, remain substantially unchanged throughout the centuries. And the patristic definition of this malign spirit— man's most pernicious vice (Basil, p. 463)—endures.

In the late medieval Sins tradition, a thousand years after Cyprian and Basil, Deadly Envy is the "werst of alle synnes." And slander is pre-eminently, although not exclusively, envious. The sense of a peculiar affinity between detraction and Envy prevails in medieval sermon, manual and mirror and in poetic allegory. In representative popular religious disquisitions on the Sins, like those in *The Book of Vices and Virtues* (a fourteenth-century adaptation of the *Somme le Roi* of Lorens d'Orleans [1279]) and *Jacob's Well* (fifteenth century), detraction is the speech of Envy. And Envy, now formally the great opposite of Love and the Sin against the Holy Ghost, is "werst of alle synnes." Why? "for othere synnes arn contrarye to on vertew, as pride is contrarye to lownesse ... but enuye is contrarye to alle vertuys and to alle goodnessis" (*Jacob's Well*, p. 82). In these treatises the Deadly Sin is divided into enviousness of heart, word, and deed; each of these categories is in turn tri-partite. The signally invidious feelings are "Schrewed Gladnesse" and its complement, grief over the joy of others. The envious man is like the basilisk, "a worm that suffreth no grene thing aboute hym, in graas, in busche, ne in tree."[22] "Livida lingua" has various sub-divisions: "Cursednesse," "Bitternesse," and "Treasoun" (from Psalm 10:7) in one treatise, "Missaying," "Bitternesse," and "Bacbyting" in the other. "Missaying" is speaking ill of another's good. It is 'Bitternesse" when "thou heryst euyl of another man, and thou makyst it more, and dost it be knowyn abowtyn ..." (*Jacob's Well*, p. 83). And out of envious "Treasoun" a man turns all the good he hears or sees "into euele and harm, and jugeth falsly" (*Vices and Virtues*, p. 23). Or he backbites, perhaps sowing "Dyscorde"; "that is, whanne thou makyst hem enemyes that were freendys, and makyst stryif and debate wyth talys and lesynges berynge aboute" (*Jacob's Well*, p. 83). The invidious man speaks ill of his fellow as "sum hownd, beforn a man, fawnyth hym wyth his tayl, and behynde him byteth hym" (*Jacob's Well*, p. 83). Significantly, even when evil speaking is treated in connection with other Deadly Sins, language and images conventionally associated with envy are used. The "mysseyer" who appears under Gluttony (Sins of the Tongue) is likened to the "manere addre

16

that is cleped saryne and that renneth faster than any hors and otherwhile thei flen, and thei beth so venemous that no triacle may saue a man that they enuenymen, for the deth cometh so sodenly after the bitynge that a man may not be holpe" (*Vices and Virtues*, p. 59). To "missay" is to imitate the hyena, the hoopoe, and the beetle that flees the "floures and loueth the dong of an hors or a best" (*Vices and Virtues*, p. 59). The detractor motivated by Gluttony seems to agree with praise of another but then says "yit . . . there is a fawte that me forthynkyth," and "thus, thrugh a pryve envie, he takyth a bytt" (*Jacob's Well*, p. 151). We are enjoined to avoid the sub-sin of Wrath called Malice of the Mouth: " . . . bakbiteth noght, weryth noght . . . steryth non other out of here charyte!" (*Jacob's Well*, p. 92). However classified, slander is associated in these treatises primarily with Satan's malevolence. And this is equally true in the great medieval poems by Gower and Lydgate which contributed to the Elizabethan artists' images of these evils.

To both Gower's *Mirour de l'Omme* and his *Confessio Amantis* the Sins tradition is central. Madeleine Doran has reminded us that Lowes concluded "with a high degree of probability that Spenser knew and used the *Mirour*," and that the *Confessio* was available in print to Elizabethans (in editions of 1483, 1543, and 1554).[23] This poetry, then, along with Chaucer's and Lydgate's representations of the Seven Sins, is part of the aesthetic background of Shakespeare and his contemporaries. Gower's Sins are arresting figures whose diverse origins he points to in his text. References to authorities like Aristotle, Isaiah, St. Paul, Horace, and Chrysostom are interlaced within allegory like that of the manuals. Gower refers with one stroke to "Jerome, Tulles, et Aristote."[24] He is considerably indebted to the two Latin poets who were most popular during the Middle Ages, Virgil and "sage Ovide" (*Mirour*, 14090); he paraphrases Seneca, Quintilian, and Martial. All these names, studding Gower's surface along with those of prophets, disciples and Church Fathers, give his poetry special amplitude. His Seven Deadly Sins are vivid and imposing.

The *Mirour* and the *Confessio*, like the theological treatises, convey the general sense that Envy, the great foe of Charity, is crucially different from the other Sins. It is "the werst vice of alle," states the Confessor.[25] Of all the Sins, all Satan's daughters, this one resembles her parent most closely "because neither night nor day does her heart slacken with regard to others' ill, but rather is she always desirous of putting others' good to ruin" (*Mirour*, 3712-14). Although Pride is the captain of the Vices and was the original cause of Satan's fall, it is Envy that is the primordial foe of God and still man's worst enemy: "le dragon malvois et viel" (*Mirour*, 3741), the "accuser" of fraternal love (*Mirour*, 3737).[26] As the manuals distinguish

17

between the other Sins, which oppose particular Virtues, and Envy, which is contrary to "alle vertuys and to alle goodnessis," so Gower underlines the uniqueness of Envy.

> . . . every vice
> Som cause hath, wherof it groweth,
> Bot of Envie noman knoweth
> Fro whenne he cam bot out of helle.

(Confessio, II.3132-35)

Envy is enigmatic, irrational and self-destructive, " . . . hath the propre kinde of helle, / Without cause to misdo / Toward himself and othre also" (*Confessio*, I. 3442-44). And Gower points to its special menace: it renders virtue helpless. "Men of prowess defend themselves from the Devil, but not at all from Envy" (*Mirour*, 3790-91); it destroys the very best of men by razing their honor (*Mirour*, 3835-40). The traditional polarization between Envy and Charity is part of the structure of the *Mirour*, and Gower also insists upon it in the dialogue of the *Confessio*. The Confessor warns the Lover against "Envie, which is loveles" (*Confessio*, II. 2961). He charges, " . . . if thou wolt in grace stonde / With love, thou most leve Envie" (*Confessio*, II. 202-03). He spells out the old opposition: "Ayein Envie is Charite, / Which is the Moder of Pite, / That makth a mannes herte tendre . . . " (*Confessio*, II. 3173-75).

Gower's images for Envy are inherited, familiar, but not yet timeworn. The principal figures, of the nettle, the serpent, and fire, tend to fuse, as here, in the nettle that stings and burns bitterly: [Envy is]

> celle urtie mal poignant,
> Que d'amertume vait bruillant
> La rose qui luy est voisine.

(Mirour, 3721-23)

We think back to the Roman poets and Plutarch, ahead to Don John. Gower turns Ovid's Envy into a serpent more pernicious than any other beast,

> Q'estaignt et tolt de sa nature
> Du fuil et herbe la verdure:
> En tous les lieus u qu'il demure
> Riens est qui soit fructefiable.

(Mirour, 3750-53)

This deadly exhalation demolishes "Honour, bonté, sen et mesure / De ses voisins" (*Mirour*, 3755-56). Like Etna, it is "ever burning but able to consume only itself" (*Mirour*, 3805-07); the Lover in the *Confessio* admits that when he sees another person happy in love,

> Ethna, which brenneth yer be yere,
> Was thanne noght so hot as I
> Of thilke Sor which prively
> Min hertes thoght withinne brenneth.

> (*Confessio*, II. 20-23)

The fire rages through the heart, leaving behind no love, not one "goute de liquor, / Dont charité soit arousée" (*Mirour*, 3827-28).

Gower divides Envy into Detraction, Sorrow for Others' Joy, Joy for Others' Grief, Supplanting, and False Seeming. Grief for Others' Joy, attended by Dissension, will make sacrifices in order to damage another (*Mirour*, 3101-02). Another's joy fills her with pain, an evil burning. She wishes to be honored above anyone else (*Mirour*, 3034-36, 3055-57) and in this is like her sister Supplanting. She will be punished in Hell, where sadness endures endlessly (*Mirour*, 3154-55). Joy for Others' Grief relishes someone else's fall (*Mirour*, 3172-74), listens to malicious talk with "joyous ear" (*Mirour*, 3213), is delighted when another is unjustly defamed (*Mirour*, 3217-22). This "Schrewed Gladnesse" in the *Confessio* is illustrated by the story of the travellers and the angel, in which the envious traveller chooses to lose one of his eyes in order that his companion suffer doubly, by losing two. Shakespeare's Don John mistakenly attributes his own "Schrewed Gladnesse" to others: "Their cheer is the greater that I am subdued" (I.iii.75).

Supplanting is a face of Envy which haunts the court, the marketplace, the Church; a male figure in the *Confessio*, he sets his heart on great offices:

> Thus goth he with his sleyhte aboute
> To hindre and schowve an other oute
> And stonden with his slyh compas
> In stede there an other was;
> And so to sette himselven inne,
> He reccheth noght, be so he winne,
> Of that an other man schal lese. . . .

> (*Confessio*, II. 2339-45)

He desires the "evil of others, until he can finally have what they had before" (*Mirour*, 3320-22). With its two poles—the wish that another lose and the desire for one's own gain—Supplanting is less purely gratuitous than its coordinate vices. This relatively worldly form of Envy is attended by Ambition, Circumvention, and Confusion.

19

False Seeming, because duplicitous, is effective when all the other daughters of Envy fail to bring evil about. Double-tongued like Detraction, False Seeming speaks fair while thinking ill, makes what is sweet bitter, turns white into black. She pretends love while hiding envy, like Judas; kills with a venomed kiss and then laughs while seeming to mourn (*Mirour*, 3495-501). False Seeming's constant companion is Hypocrisy, "Whos word descordeth to his thoght: / Forthi thei ben togedre broght / Of o covine, of on houshold..." (*Confessio*, II. 1893-95). When Envy wishes to deceive, she sends Hypocrisy, "For whan his semblant is most clier, / Thanne is he most derk in his thoght..." (*Confessio*, II. 1918-19). Gower opposes the countenance to the heart in describing Hypocrisy:

> Thogh men him se, thei knowe him noght;
> Bot as it scheweth in the glas
> Thing which therinne nevere was
> So sheweth it in his visage
> That nevere was in his corage:
> Thus doth he al his thing with sleyhte.

(Confessio, II. 1920-25)

We remember Basil's observation that the envious hide their true feelings, and we think of the false faces of Shakespeare's slanderers, especially the mask which covers Iago's dark thoughts. Says the Confessor, "my Sone, if thou be wys, / Do no viser upon thi face, / Which as wol noght thin herte embrace" (*Confessio*, II. 2080-82).

But Detraction is Envy's eldest daughter and is worse than all the others. This is the specific enemy of "the harmony which is created by love" (*Mirour*, 2730); it is the force which destroys trust, drives people apart, and threatens all social coherence. Root and branch evil, so alike, seem to coalesce; the poet adapts Ovid to delineate Detraction:

> For as the Netle which up renneth
> The freisshe rede Roses brenneth
> And makth hem fade and pale of hewe,
> Riht so this fals Envious hewe,
> In every place wher he duelleth,
> With false wordes which he telleth
> He torneth preisinge into blame
> And worschipe into worldes schame.

(Confessio, II. 401-08)

The ruin of a person's good name is more grievous than loss of possessions.[27] When one's fame is destroyed, it cannot be restored (*Mirour*, 2841-42, 2913-

16). Suddenly through defamation "the renown of a good vassal for all time changes" (*Mirour*, 2854-56); only a special grace can rescue the victim from his enemy (*Mirour*, 2650-52). Slander moves like a serpent in the grass:

> Qant hom le touche, tout ensi
> Detractour d'enviouse dent
> Mordt en secré la bonne gent.
>
> (*Mirour*, 2643-45)

Like the Siren, the serpent that outruns any horse, slander kills with its venomous breath before one can feel the evil (*Mirour*, 2845-56). The detractor resembles the hoopoe, the dung beetle, the hound (*Mirour*, 2893-97). A slanderer in the *Confessio* does in prison like a dog, "Which lich was of condicioun, / Whan he with his detraccioun / Bark on his brother so behinde" (*Confessio*, II. 1859-61). The poisoned well (*Confessio*, II. 565), the swift arrow (*Mirour*, 2833-37), the double-edged sword (*Mirour*, 2785-86)[28] stand for an evil which secretly destroys good and bad alike, attacks "piere et miere et soer germeine, / Moigne, Frere, Canoun, Noneine, / Prestre, Clerc, Reclus, Hermite, / Les grans seignours, la gent petite" (*Mirour*, 2740-43). Detraction is characterized further, through secondary allegory, by a retinue of confederates and assistants. Malbouche, the foremost, not only recites all the evil he knows of but fabricates it "Du mal qu'il tient en son demeine" (*Mirour*, 2747-49). From one word he will invent a whole story "de sa malice propre" (*Mirour*, 2694). Where he goes, Disfame always follows, and with Disfame inevitably are "Reproef" and "Vituperie," taking away from a man his good name and the good opinion his fellows have of him. Thus Gower's Detraction is most like the Deadly Sin which engenders it, as it labors so insidiously against the goodness in people and the love that ties them together. "And many a worthi love is grieved / Thurgh bacbitinge of false Envie" (*Confessio*, II. 450-51).

Chaucer's Parson's disquisition on Envy, disorderly and flat compared with Gower's treatment, contains the essentials of the traditional definition. Lydgate's early fifteenth-century *Pilgrimage of the Life of Man*, "one of the moral poems which presumably formed a part of Spenser's wide background of reading,"[29] includes analyses of all the Sins and sub-sins. Lydgate's vision of his characters is more dramatic than Gower's definitions and his formal treatment a step closer to Spenser's, the *Pilgrimage* being, like Book One of *The Faerie Queene*, a spiritual journey. The pilgrim narrator is assailed by Envy and her two daughters, Treason and Detraction. Wrath of Others' Prosperity and Joy of their Adversity are now two poison-shedding spears that come out of Envy's eyes. Envy introduces herself to the pilgrim:

21

> 'I am that beste serpentyne,
> Wych, off entent, my sylff enclyne,
> With alle ffolkys to debaate;
> Ande alle ffolkys ek I Haate;
> I loue no thyng (thys the cas)
> Hih nor lowe, hault nor baas,
> In hevene, erthe, nor in the se;
> I ha despyt off charyte,
> And ek also, in every cost,
> I werreye euery maner whyht;
> I taake noon heed off wrong nor ryht,
> Reward off no man alyue.'[80]

The essentials of the traditional configuration are here: the opposition to love, the alignment against humanity out of sheer indiscriminate spite, the enmity to the Holy Ghost. The pilgrim completes the characterization by describing—in Ovidian manner—the appearance of this "beste serpentyne":

> Megre and lene, off chere and look;
> And for verray Ire she shook,
> Dreye as a bast, voyde off blood,
> Hyr fflessh wastyd, (and thus yt stood,)
> Men myghte sen bothe nerffe and bon,
> And hyr Ioyntes euerychon.   (14775-780)

Treason and Detraction speak their pieces. Treason has a veil and holds a knife behind her back. It is she that the Devil has taught to imitate the scorpion, to look cheerful while stinging people in the back. She is like

> the serpent
> Wych, vnder herbys fressh and soote,
> Ys wont to daren by the roote,
> Coueryd with many a lusty fflour.   (15158-61)

Detraction, Envy's other daughter, has her customary grudge against the world. She asks the pilgrim how he dares to hold a staff, avowing,

> 'I haate stavys euerychon,
> Off pylgrymes, whan they gon
> On pylgrymage wher they wende,
> Whan they be crossyd At the ende.
> In hem I ffynde alway som lak,
> and berke at hem behynde her bak. . . .'   (15277-82)

Detraction tells the pilgrim that she and Envy plan to eat him; but he feels safe, having done nothing to incur infamy. Detraction points out that virtue is no protection against defamation:

> '. . . I make ay som resoun
> By fals Interpretacioun,
> What good werk I se men do.
> Wyn in-to water I chaunge also;
> I tourne ek by collusioun
> Tryacle to venym and poysoun.
> Worshepe I tourne in-to dyffame;
> On folkys goode, I putte ay blame;
> Ther goode name, in halle and boure,
> As Rawh fflessh I kan devoure.'   (15333-44)

She takes away a man's good name with her flesh-hook and feeds it to Envy: "Thys secounde cours (yt ys no dred,) / Doth gret good vn-to hyr hed; . . . ffor wych I am mad 'cusyner,' / And for hyr mouth, 'cheff potager' " (15434-44).[31] Detraction utters her traditional boast that while Hell cannot injure the holy, she can hurt anyone with false report,

> 'ffor there ys noon so good alyve,
> Nor neuere was, in-to thys day,
> But that I koude fynde a way,
> Hys name and hys vertues alle,
> ffor tapeyre hem or apalle,
> By som fals wynd reysed aloffte.'   (15480-85)

The white dove alights on the pilgrim and saves him from his enemies. Lydgate is an important antecedent to Spenser because he combines homiletic allegory and story. His Sins are vital characters, more naturalistically convincing than Gower's are meant to be. And the malice which Lydgate's Envy and Detraction feel toward the pilgrim with the cross, we shall see, is the same as Archimago's hatred of the Red Cross Knight.

The Sixteenth Century

The configuration comprised of Deadly Envy and its sub-sins is no less commonplace in Shakespeare's century. "Of all other vices in the worlde," writes Geoffrey Fenton in 1575, "enuie is the most auncient, of most custome, and of greatest continuaunce, yea euen to the ende of the world. It tooke beginning in the serpent."[32] And slander is still the "ranke poyson of the Diuell,"[33] Envy's most dreadful weapon. The old personifications appear everywhere. Sir Thomas More's discussion of the Seven Deadly Sins in *A Treatise of the Four Last Things* (1522) includes a mainly Ovidian Envy, with Horace's Sicilian tyrants and Gower's "burning hill of Etna" blended smoothly in: "For surely envy is such a torment as all the tyrants of Sicily never devised a sorer. And it so drinketh up the moisture of the body and consumeth the good blood, so discoloureth the face, so defaceth the beauty, so disfigureth the visage, leaving it all bony, lean, pale, and wan, that a person well set awork with envy needeth none other image of death than his own face in a glass . . . as the fire of the burning hill of Etna burneth only itself, so doth the envious person fret, fume, and burn in his own heart. . . . "[34] The ancient images are reiterated throughout the Tudor era from the pulpit and elsewhere in theological discussion; Bishop Pilkington writes in 1585 about the sin which is "worse than any poison of other beasts," illustrating with snake, adder, canker, consumption.[35] Golding's translation of *Metamorphoses* in 1567 may have brought the figurative tradition fresh popularity; Elizabethan representations of Envy are usually distinctly Roman. Whitney's "Invidiae descriptio" derives, the marginal notation indicates, from Ovid and Lucretius:

> What meanes her eies?   so bleared, sore, and redd:
> Her mourninge still, to see an others gaine.
> And what is mente by snakes vpon her head?
> The fruite that springes, of such a venomed braine.
> But whie, her harte shee rentes within her brest?
> It shewes her selfe, doth worke her owne vnrest.[36]

In the 1590's Lodge presents the sins of his London in the semi-allegorical pamphlet, *Wits Miserie*. Alice Walker deduces that this "must have been written with a small library at his elbow"; one of the sources was the *Somme des Pechez (Somme le Roi)*.[37] Rosamond Tuve notes that Lodge's Sins are thoroughly traditional: "He calls the 'amitie' who counters envy, 'love', as did the English *Somme le roi*. . . . The sub-sins each devil has in his train would make us think very little time had elapsed since Alanus, if we had not met them so often since the 1160's."[38] Lodge gives "BELZEBUB the enuious, grand God of flies," three sons.[39] Worldly Fear is much like Gower's Supplantation in his jealousy of others' successes and his fear of equals in office (p. 59). Hate-Vertue is "Sorrow for another mans good successe," and he is the one who, his tongue "tipt with lying, his heart steeld against charity, . . . walks for the most part in black vnder colour of grauity, and looks as pale as the Visard of ye ghost which cried so miserally at ye Theator like an oister wife, *Hamlet, reuenge*: he is full of infamy and slander, insomuch as if he ease not his stomack in detracting somwhat or some man before noontide, he fals into a feuer that holds him while supper time. . . ." He "grumbles, murmures continually, although nothing crosse him" (p. 56). His brother "Malitious Hatred" is, of course, he whose "felicity is to rejoice at other mens harms." "Malitious Hatred" is like Cyprian's envier: "This fellow still walks with his hat ouer his eies, confirming that of IOHN, He y^t hateth his brother liueth in darknes. If a man offend him, he admits no reconcilement" (p. 58). Distributed among the children of Lodge's Envy are all the important traits.

A different kind of characterization, equally indebted to the traditional complex, comes from Sidney's *Arcadia*. From the conventional material Sidney creates a realistic councillor, "a man of the most envious disposition, that (I think) ever infected the aire with his breath: whose eies could not looke right upon any happie man, nor eares bear the burthen of any bodies praise: contrary to the natures of al other plagues, plagued with others well being; making happines the ground of his unhappinesse, and good newes the argument of his sorrow: in sum, a man whose favour no man could winne, but by being miserable."[40] Sidney's debt to the Sins tradition is inconspicuous; the physical details of breath and eyes and the spiritual categories seem natural. That the writer uses the old pattern so unobtrusively is an indication of the extent to which it permeates his imaginative environment.

Jacobeans demonstrate that custom has continued to perpetuate, though not yet staled, the traditional formulation. Chapman in *Bussy d'Ambois* (1607) echoes post-classical treatments, and Lydgate's description. His Envy, gluttonous,

> feeds on outcast entrails like a kite;
> In which foul heap, if any ill lies hid,
> She sticks her beak into it, shakes it up,
> And hurls it all abroad, that all may view it.
> Corruption is her nutriment; but touch her
> With any precious ointment, and you kill her.
> Where she finds any filth in men, she feasts,
> And with her black throat bruits it through the world
> Being sound and healthful; but if she but taste
> The slenderest pittance of commended virtue,
> She surfeits of it, and is like a fly
> That passes all the body's soundest parts,
> And dwells upon the sores; or if her squint eye
> Have power to find none there, she forges some.[41]

Finally, this from Middleton in 1618, brings together comparisons not rare, but resonant: "Envy! Oh what does that *ulcus animae* amongst us? That Etna in a man, that continually burns itself, *intus et extra*, within and without; that like the cantharides found feeding on the fairest and flourishing roses, so envy is ever opposed against the most sweet, noble, flourishing, and peaceful blossoms. Were she as rare as the comparison, I could call her Phoenix, and wish that this day she would burn herself, and leave the ashes issueless."[42]

25

The inveterate association between Envy and detraction is still axiomatic. Baldwin writes, in *A Treatise of Morall Philosophy*, 1547 (a book which went through more editions in sixteenth-century England than any other except the Bible):

> Enuie and slander are two mischieuous vices,
> And knit still in vaine to a wicked end,
> To defame or kill they are full of deuises,
> They regard none estate be he foe or friend
>
> .... (p. 277)

"Enuie and ill tongues"[43] still belong together; Envie is still seen "Feeding on Slaunder";[44] the "brood of Enuy" continue to spread "slaunderous report."[45] No less than ever is Envy the "canker of honor,"[46] "to honor sworne a secret foe."[47] Detraction is still "Enuies abhorred child";[48] as always Truth laments that Envy is her malicious enemy.[49] But even when dissociated from the Deadly Sin, detraction, states the Elizabethan as clearly as had his medieval predecessor, "hurteth charitie, when it disseuereth friends asunder, and bringeth them into dissention and hatred...."[50] This "venemous euill," Baldwin writes, "or ranke poyson of the Diuell, is poured by him into the hearts onely of wicked and malicious men, who ... [spare not] to blow out with euill-fauoured and stinking breaths, the very shamefull and hurtfull blasts of slanderous and euill reports; whereby euen the very godly are of their good name and fame impayred, their estimation discredited, their friends abated, their welfare much hindered, and their ioyes here so shaken in this life, that they are driuen with bitter teares to cry vnto God for helpe, and to be deliuered of such their cursed detractors" (p. 321). The sense that slander breaks "the bond of that most incomparable vertue of Amity" (p. 325) is as strong in the Renaissance as ever before.

From an analysis of the Ten Commandments by Thomas Becon, probably written during King Edward's reign, comes an examination of the significance of name and the ethical seriousness of false witness.[51] To explain the ninth commandment Becon cites the familiar scriptural passages, with figures of poison, fire, sword and arrow; he refers to the story of the "virtuous and chaste lady Susanna." He warns that not only false witness-bearing and lying are forbidden by the commandment, but also "slandering, evil reporting, backbiting, defaming of our neighbour, with all other vices of the tongue." His sub-divisions remind us of the allegorical system: with false witness are associated the privy accuser, the man who creates strife ("For an angry man kindleth variance, and the ungodly disquieteth friends, and putteth discord among them that be at peace"), and "bitterness," "fierceness," "wrath," "roaring," "cursed speaking," and "maliciousness."

After taking up what the ninth commandment forbids, Becon explores what it requires, so that "we may learn to know and to do [God's] will and pleasure." While his structure is different from that of the disquisitions on the vices and virtues, the Renaissance homilist also places sin and virtue in antithetical relation. His system of contrasts points up, as clearly as had medieval allegory, detraction's enmity to love. The full social significance of the sins of the tongue becomes explicit as Becon explains the positive obligations implicit in the ninth commandment. The Lord requires, first, that we "boldly and without fear . . . testify the truth"; secondly, that we speak well of our neighbor, "defend his good name, set forth his good report, maintain his honest estimation." Thirdly, we must not only refrain from slander but also help to reconcile those who are in dissension, "to make them friends, to set them at one, and to link them together again in true amity and unfeigned love." (One thinks of Desdemona's attempts to mend the friendship between Cassio and Othello, broken by the slanderer). And fourthly, we are to "set forth the glory of God and the commodity of our neighbour." Becon's analysis of divine law displays forcefully the old opposition between slander and peace. So do Spenser's legends of perfect knighthood.

The Faerie Queene

Even if the whole tradition were not so pervasive in sixteenth-century literature, *The Faerie Queene* would demonstrate its continuing vitality. In Faerieland there is no evil deadlier than slander; Spenser makes it the enemy of Holiness, Love, and Courtesy. Archimago in Book One, Ate and Duessa in Book Four, and the Blatant Beast all embody, variously, the traditional conception. And Spenser's personifications of Enuie, Sclaunder, and Detraction themselves are classic.

Archimago, in terms of the plot the villain of Book One even though the dragon is the object of the Red Cross Knight's quest, is (among much else, of course) a representation of Envy. His wish to destroy Una springs from devilish malice:

> For her he hated as the hissing snake,
> And in her many troubles did most pleasure take.[52]

He is the natural enemy of Holiness and Truth, and his goal is to keep them separated. Slander is his characteristic weapon; he fakes evidence that Una is "a loose Leman to vile seruice bound" (I.i.48). He teaches a spirit from the underworld to "imitate that lady Trew, / Whose semblance she did carrie under feigned hew" (I.i.46). And the Knight of Holiness, suspicious of the spirit's truth but too innocent ("since no'vntruth he knew" [I.i.53]) to penetrate the disguise, ends up "Much grieu'd to thinke that gentle Dame so light, / For whose defence he was to shed his blood" (I.i.55). Next Archimago places the artificial "Una" in bed with a manufactured young Squire. The deceiver, his "seeming" false,

> . . . runnes with feigned faithfull hast
> Vnto his guest . . .
> And to him cals, Rise rise vnhappy Swaine,
> That here wex old in sleepe, whiles wicked wights
> Haue knit themselues in *Venus* shamefull chain;
> Come see, where your false Lady doth her honour staine.

(I.ii.4)

With this deception the "bold bad man" (I.i.37) whose religious guise camouflages active malice against Una and her Knight, does separate them into "double parts." And he congratulates himself on the "diuelish arts, / That had such might ouer true meaning harts" (I.ii.9). He succeeds for a time in leaving innocence mistaken and helpless. And even after the Red Cross Knight has overcome the deceiver and accomplished his mission, Archimago works in envy against his honor:

> And now exceeding griefe him ouercame,
> To see the *Redcrosse* thus aduaunced hye;
> Therefore this craftie engine he did frame,
> Against his praise to stirre vp enmitye
> Of such, as vertues like mote vnto him allye.

(II.i.23)

Again slander is aimed against amity as Archimago accuses the Red Cross Knight to Guyon: "Loe yonder he, cryde Archimago alowd, / That wrought the shamefull fact, which I did shewe" (II.i.25). After suddenly recognizing Holiness, Guyon explains his mistake:

> A false infamous faitor late befell
> Me for to meet, that seemed ill bested,
> And playnd of grieuous outrage, which he red
> A knight had wrought against a Ladie gent;
> Which to auenge, he to this place me led.

(II.i.30)

28

We recognize in Archimago the traditional facets of Envy. Ill will toward others in their griefs and joys, false seeming, and detraction work actively against the protagonists of Book One. As Iago will, Spenser's villain leads a knight to debase himself and so actually deserve infamy:

> For all he did, was to deceiue good knights,
>> And draw them from pursuit of praise and fame,
>> To slug in slouth and sensuall delights,
>> And end their daies with irrenowmned shame.

(II.i.23)

Upton called Archimago "the common enemy," "the adversary, the accuser, the deceiver,"[53] and Greenlaw saw in him a representation of Satan.[54] Spenser suggests the identification by naming his villain "cunning Architect of cancred guile" (II.i.1). But Archimago need not be the Devil himself even though his spirit is satanic; his feelings, attitudes, and actions are devilish as Deadly Envy is devilish. He is a human portrayal of the abstraction Spenser personifies, in the parade of the Seven Deadly Sins, as hater of "all good workes and vertuous deeds." Here is the Sin:

> ... malicious *Enuie* rode,
>> Vpon a rauenous wolfe, and still did chaw
>> Betweene his cankred teeth a venemous tode,
>> That all the poison ran about his chaw;
>> But inwardly he chawed his owne maw
>> At neighbours wealth, that made him euer sad;
>> For death it was, when any good he saw,
>> And wept, that cause of weeping none he had,
> But when he heard of harme, he wexed wondrous glad.
>
> All in a kirtle of discolourd say
>> He clothed was, ypainted full of eyes;
>> And in his bosome secretly there lay
>> An hatefull Snake, the which his taile vptyes
>> In many folds, and mortall sting implyes.
>> Still as he rode, he gnasht his teeth, to see
>> Those heapes of gold with griple Couetyse,
>> And grudged at the great felicitie
> Of proud *Lucifera*, and his owne companie.
>
> He hated all good workes and vertuous deeds,
>> And him no lesse, that any like did vse,
>> And who with gracious bread the hungry feeds,
>> His almes for want of faith he doth accuse;
>> So euery good to bad he doth abuse:
>> And eke the verse of famous Poets witt

> He does backebite, and spightfull poison spues
> From leprous mouth on all, that euer writt:
> Such one vile *Enuie* was, that fifte in row did sitt.
>
> (I.iv.30-32)

The detail is perfectly traditional. Envy's self-destructiveness is epitomized, with profound irony, by his resentment of the other Sins' "advantages," Deadly Couetyse his deadly gold, Lucifera her mortal "felicitie."

Slander is structurally important in Book Four; it is the adversary of social concord, of love and good will. The most dedicated villains in the Book of Friendship are Ate and Duessa, two who are not the ladies they seem,

> albee in face
> And outward shew fair semblance they did beare;
> For vnder maske of beautie and good grace,
> Vile treason and fowle falshood hidden were,
> That mote to none but to the warie wise appeare.
>
> (IV.i.17)

Duessa, who can "forge all colours, saue the trew" (IV.i.18), epitomizes false seeming. She has called up from hell Ate, the one "most fit to trouble noble knights, / Which hunt for honor" (IV.i.19). Ate is "mother of debate, / And all dissention, which doth dayly grow / Amongst fraile men, that many a publike state / And many a priuate oft doth ouerthrow" (IV.i.19). Together they work to separate friends and lovers, to shatter society itself. Usually, their instrument is slander.

Ate, Discord, is much like Envy. We remember that in *Jacob's Well* "Sowyng of Dyscorde" ("whanne thou makyst hem enemyes that were freendys, and makyst stryif and debate with talys and lesynges berynge aboute" [p. 83] was a subdivision of envious Bacbyting. The associations are still customary. In a pageant Holinshed describes, "The chief instruments of discord, namelie, Enuie and Slander, . . . peered out behind, Enuie gnawing hir owne heart, and Slander hauing double heart, double toong, and double face, howbeit with small effect."[55] Spenser's Discord is envious:

> . . . life it is to her, when others sterue
> Through mischieuous debate, and deadly feood. . . .
>
> (IV.i.26)

Her face is familiar, "With squinted eyes contrarie wayes intended,

> And loathly mouth, vnmeete a mouth to bee,
> That nought but gall and venim comprehended,
> And wicked wordes that God and man offended.

30

And she takes in Gower's False Seeming and False Thinking:

> Her lying tongue was in two parts diuided,
> And both the parts did speake, and both contended;
> And as her tongue, so was her hart discided,
> That neuer thoght one thing, but doubly stil was guided.
>
> (IV.i.27)

She also represents the wickedness of believing falsehood, an evil Spenser warns against in Book Two (II.xi.10); her ears are "Fild with false rumours" (IV.i.28). Like Envy, Discord "sought to bring all things vnto decay / For all her study was and all her thought, / How she might ouerthrow the things that Concord wrought" (IV.i.29). She is like Satan and Archimago in her sheer malice, hatred of goodness, alignment against the divine scheme:

> So much her malice did her might surpas,
>   That euen th'Almightie selfe she did maligne,
>   Because to man so mercifull he was,
>   And vnto all his creatures so benigne,
>   Sith she her selfe was of his grace indigne:
>   For all this worlds faire workmanship she tride,
>   Vnto his last confusion to bring,
>   And that great golden chaine quite to diuide,
> With which it blessed Concord hath together tide.
>
> (IV.i.30)

This book of *The Faerie Queene* is a demonstration that true love "of honor and all vertue is / The roote, and brings forth glorious flowres of fame, / That crowne true louers with immortall bliss" (Proem.2). "Spenser conceives of friendship as a harmonizing and unifying principle of cosmic love operating in the realm of man to promote concord."[56] It is all this that Ate sets herself against when she tries to ruin Scudamour's faith in his beloved, Amoret, and his friend, Britomart. That detraction is the weapon of her choice serves to point up the power of slander over love.

She tells Scudamour that Amoret loves another knight, "with whom she now goth / In louely wise, and sleepes, and sports, and playes." We know from the outset that the "knight" is really a lady, so there is comic irony in the whole story. But the victim's suspicion and jealousy are no less real for being absurd. After Ate tells him,

> I saw him haue your *Amoret* at will,
> I saw him kisse, I saw him her embrace,
> I saw him sleepe with her all night his fill,

31

> And manie nights, and manie by in place,
> That present were to testifie the case.

$$(IV.i.47-49)$$

he is convinced. He condemns the "knight" to whom Amoret has been
entrusted:

> Discourteous,   disloyall *Britomart*,
> Vntrue to God, and vnto man vniust,
> What vengeance due can equall thy desart,
> That hast with shamefull spot of sinfull lust
> Defil'd the pledge committed to thy trust?

That Britomart is the precise opposite of all these things as the Knight of
Chastity, perfect in loyalty, truth, and justice, ironically underlines the swift
efficiency of malicious falsehood. The deceived lover throws at her name the
worst oath: "Let vgly shame and endlesse infamy / Color thy name with
foule reproaches rust" (IV.i.53). When Britomart's nurse, Glauce, tries to
assuage Scudamour's "flaming furie" and to clear Britomart, he almost kills
her. Discord reigns indeed.

Spenser's study of this young man afflicted with unfounded jealousy and
care emphasizes the evil of false accusation. Like Leontes, he can find "Nor
night nor day no rest." A once gentle person now filled by the "incarnate
deuill" Ate, he is tortured by thoughts of revenge:

> Bent to reuenge on blameless *Britomart*
> The crime, which cursed Ate kindled earst,
> The which like thornes did pricke his gealous hart,
> And through his soule like poysoned arrow perst,
> That by no reason it might be reuerst,
> The more it gauld, and grieu'd him night and day,
> That nought but dire reuenge his anger mote defray.

$$(IV.v.31)$$

Glauce attempts to reason with the knight, as characters in *The Winter's Tale*
will with Leontes: but the stubbornness of false suspicion is itself a theme.
The "thornes," "poysoned arrow," and gall in Scudamour's heart and soul
point to the malice responsible for his grief. In this slander story, Spenser
accentuates how easily the malicious lie can dissolve peace. "What equall
torment to the griefe of mind, / And pyning anguish hid in gentle hart, /
That inly feeds it selfe with thoughts vnkind, / And nourisheth her owne
consuming smart?" (IV.vi.1).

Spenser depicts Sclaunder herself in his tale of Friendship. She is

32

A foule and loathly creature sure in sight,
  And in conditions to be loath'd no lesse:
For she was stuft with rancour and despight
  Vp to the throat, that oft with bitternesse
  It forth would breake, and gush in great excesse,
  Pouring out streames of poyson and of gall
  Gainst all, that truth or vertue doe professe,
  Whom she with leasings lewdly did miscall,
And wickedly backbite. . . .

Her nature is all goodnesse to abuse,
  And causelesse crimes continually to frame,
  With which she guiltlesse persons may accuse,
  And steale away the crowne of their good name;
  Ne euer Knight so bold, ne euer Dame
  So chast and loyall liu'd, but she would striue
  With forged cause them falsely to defame;
  Ne euer thing so well was doen aliue,
But she with blame would blot, and of due praise
                    depriue.   (IV.viii.24-25)

Arthur, Amoret and Aemylia stay in Sclaunder's cottage for a night and are not harmed. They "endured all with patience milde, / . . . Regardless of that queane so base and vilde" (IV.iii.28), leaving her in the morning to rail by herself "Till she had duld the sting, which in her tongs end grew" (IV.viii.36). One critic contrasts with Scudamour's liability to false suspicion, "the suggested security against slander of Amoret and Aemylia when attended by Arthur": " . . . she only illustrates an impotent rage. . . . "[57] Arthur symbolizes a world in which slander cannot work:

          . . . antique age yet in the infancie
          Of time, did liue then like an innocent,
          In simple truth and blamelesse chastitie,
          Ne then of guile had made experiment,
          But voide of vile and treacherous intent,
          Held vertue for it selfe in soueraine awe:
          Then loyall loue had royall regiment. . . .

                    (IV.iii.30)

But it is not our world, or Faerieland. Among "fraile men" falsity all too easily passes for truth, reason and language are too often perverted by ill will. Sclaunder's

          words were not, as common words are ment,
          T'express the meaning of the inward mind,
          But noysome breath, and poysnous spirit sent
          From inward parts, with cancred malice lind,

And breathed forth with blast of bitter wind;
Which passing through the eares, would pierce the hart,
And wound the soule it selfe with griefe vnkind;
For like the stings of Aspes, that kill with smart,
Her spightfull words did pricke, and wound the inner part.

(IV.viii.26)

The "blast of bitter wind" looks forward to the Blatant Beast whose breath will wound guiltless people in Book Six. Spenser opposes the "meaning of the inward mind" to "poysnous spirit sent / From inward parts" in order to emphasize the irrationality of detraction: it represents the power of a lower impulse over something higher. Detraction devastates the best in us, the love that "of honor and all vertue is / The roote. . . . "

It is in the Book of Courtesy that the slanderous spirit is most prominent, for Calidore's mission is to quell the Blatant Beast, and the Beast serves Enuie and Detraction. As Book Five comes to its close, these two appear as a pair of ill-favored hags, angry with the Knight of Justice, leading the Beast "to their purpose." Spenser describes them, Enuie first:

The one of them, that elder did appeare,
  With her dull eyes did seeme to looke askew,
  That her mis-shape much helpt; and her foule heare
  Hung loose and loathsomely: Thereto her hew
  Was wan and leane, that all her teeth arew,
  And all her bones might through her cheekes be red;
  Her lips were raw lether, pale and blew,
  And as she spake, therewith she slauered;
Yet spake she seldom, but thought more, the lesse she sed.

(V.xii.29)

The traditional appearance, mannerisms, and spiritual traits are presented in three more stanzas, dense with the staple words and images whose histories spring immediately to mind. Enuie gnaws on a snake, drips gore and poison, eats her own gall. Her "long nayles" recall Basil's vulture, for they are like "puttocks claws." This stanza on her sorrows and joys, while distinctly Elizabethan, looks back across fifteen centuries:

. . . if she hapt of any good to heare,
  That had to any happily betid,
  Then would she inly fret and grieue, and teare
  Her flesh for felnesse, which she inward hid.
  But if she heard of ill, that any did,
  Or harme, that any had, then would she make
  Great cheare, like one vnto a banquet bid;

And in anothers losse great pleasure take,
As she had got thereby, and gayned a great stake.

(V.xii.32)

The portrait of Detraction is similarly quintessential. She is even more vicious than Enuie, who only vexes herself; "But this same both her selfe, and others eke perplext.

Her face was vgly, and her mouth distort,
  Foming with poyson round about her gils,
  In which her cursed tongue full sharpe and short
  Appear'd like Aspis sting, that closely kils,
  Or cruelly does wound, whom so she wils:
  A distaffe in her other hand she had,
  Vpon the which she little spinnes, but spils,
  And faynes to weaue false tales and leasings bad,
To throw amongst the good, which others had disprad.

(V.xii.35-36)

These, along with Spenser's descriptions of Deadly Enuie and Sclaunder, are perfect full-length portraits; the passages stand as monuments, near the end of the tradition. Now "themselues combynd in one," Enuie and Detraction have lured the Blatant Beast into their service; they rail at Justice while the Beast barks, bays, and bellows with a hundred tongues.

And euermore those hags themselues did paine,
To sharpen him, and their owne cursed tongs did straine.

(V.xii.41)

Thus slander is part of what Lewis calls the "allegorical core" of the Book of Courtesy, as an element of the Beast. Slander, Judson wrote, seems of all expressions of discourtesy "to be the most repugnant to Spenser."[58]

Whatever version of the ancestry of the Blatant Beast we accept, it comes from a family of serpent-like monsters traditionally inimical to men. In describing it Spenser again borrows from the vocabulary long associated with Envy and detraction. (As with Archimago, to identify these elements of the Blatant Beast is not to reduce the characterization to them.) The Beast conducts its warfare against courtesy with venom, poison, and gall. Brought up in hell,

Into this wicked world he forth was sent,
To be the plague and scourge of wretched men:

Whom with vile tongue and venemous intent
He sore doth wound, and bite, and cruelly torment.

(VI.i.8)

The animal seems all mouth. The hermit depicts

A wicked Monster, that his tongue doth whet
Gainst all, both good and bad, both most and least,
And poures his poysnous gall forth to infest
  The noblest wights with notable defame:
  Ne euer Knight, that bore so lofty creast,
  Ne euer Lady of so honest name,
But he them spotted with reproch, or secrete shame.

(VI.vi.12)

Spenser makes clear that injuries inflicted by this predator are the worst kind:

No wound, which warlike hand of enemy
  Inflicts with dint of sword, so sore doth light,
As doth the poysnous sting, which infamy
  Infixeth in the name of noble wight:
  For by no art, nor any leaches might
It euer can recured be again. . . .

(VI.vi.1)

The point is unfolded in the stories of two who are stung by defamation. Serena's encounter with the Beast comes about after Calidore finds her and her knight resting in the shade. "His warlike armes he had from him vndight: / For that him selfe he thought from daunger free, / And far from enuious eyes that mote him spight" (VI.iii.20). While Calidore and the Knight converse, Serena wanders off to enjoy the beauty of the day: ". . . as liking led / Her wauering lust after her wandring sight / . . . Without suspect of ill or daungers hidden dred." Suddenly "the Blatant Beast forth rushing unaware, / Caught her thus loosely wandring here and there, / And in his wide great mouth away her bare" (VI.iii.23-24). She is very seriously hurt, but her knight finds her, takes care of her wounds, and preserves her life. The Beast continues to range, and on a "straunge occasion" (VI.v.11) bites Timias. Arthur's squire has been forgiven by Belphebe for a misdemeanor and is in "happie blisse,"

Nether of enuy, nor of chaunge afeard,
Though many foes did him maligne therefore,
And with vniust detraction him did beard;

36

Yet he himselfe so well and wisely bore,
That in her soueraine lyking he dwelt euermore.

(VI.v.12)

But three "mightie enemies did him most despight, . . . That him not onely
sought by open might / To ouerthrow, but to supplant by slight." They are
Despetto, Decetto, and Defetto, and joined together, find the Blatant Beast
"the fittest meanes . . . to worke his vtter shame, and throughly him con-
found." They send the beast as a bait "To draw him from his deare beloued
dame, / Unwares into the daunger of defame" (VI.v.13-15). As they knew
he would, he challenges the monster, but it is he and not the monster who is
successful. The Beast

forced was to turne from him and fly:
Yet ere he fled, he with his tooth impure
Him heedlesse bit, the whiles he was thereof secure.

(VI.v.16)

The allegory of these incidents is complex. Characters in Faerieland who
lay down their armor, who wander "loosely," regularly encounter trouble. A
commentator wrote, "One who is blameless can afford to be indifferent, as
indeed both Artegall (1.9) and Calidore (3.16) are. But he who by a misstep
has invited slander can win back peace only by living a pure, well-disciplined,
open life."[59] But if Serena and Timias are too little aware of the hidden
danger of defamation, they are also guiltless of any moral wrong. They do not
deserve shame. This, indeed, is why slander is so ugly: it is arbitrary, it
attacks the innocent and unsuspecting. "Virtue itself 'scapes not calumnious
strokes."[60]

The hermit who tends Timias and Serena and who "knew the diuerse went
of mortall wayes, / And in the mindes of men had great insight" (V.vi.3),
finds that their wounds are past medical remedy. He explains,

. . . that beastes teeth, which wounded you tofore,
Are so exceeding venemous and keene,
Made all of rusty yron,ranckling sore,
That where they bite, it booteth not to weene
With salue, or antidote, or other mene
It euer to amend. . . .

(VI.vi.9)

"The best," the hermit says,

> that I can you aduize,
> Is to auoide the occasion of the ill:
> For when the cause, whence euill doth arize,
> Remoued is, the'effect surceaseth still.
> Abstaine from pleasure, and restraine your will.[61]

(VI.vi.9)

Serena and Timias, luckier than Desdemona, live to see their "euill plight[s]" repaired: "And eke the biting of that harmefull Beast / Was throughly heal'd." Now they at least know what the Beast is; perhaps those who have learned to fear and avoid this assailant of the courteous are less vulnerable. But Faerieland is never to be safe from it, for at the end of Calidore's story it "raungeth through the world againe,"

> Barking and biting al that him doe bate,
> Albe they worthy blame, or cleare of crime.

(VI.xii.40)

Like *Cymbeline* and *The Winter's Tale*, the Book of Courtesy opposes country to court life, giving slander a more congenial home in the latter. As C. S. Lewis pointed out, the Blatant Beast "has ravaged all the world except the shepherds."[62] Judson differentiated Spenser from most of his contemporaries who wrote on courtesy because of his tendency to treat the ideal as "essentially a matter of the heart," frequently "found far from princes' courts."[63] Allegorically central to Spenser's revelation of Courtesy are the age-old oppositions, between envy and simplicity of heart, detraction and innocence of spirit. Shakespeare's sense of the absolute evil of slander, the power of its "venom'd spear" over love, is the same.

CHAPTER TWO

Much Ado about Nothing and Garter's Susanna

The main plot of *Much Ado* becomes more clearly intelligible if we realize that Shakespeare designed it so as to throw into relief the traditional conception of slander. To achieve this emphasis he had to recast his source material completely. The Hero-Claudio plot came from writers—principally Ariosto, Bandello, Beverley, and Whetstone[1]—who, aiming at psychological verisimilitude, concentrated on the emotions of the villain, the victim, and her friends. They gave their slanderers credible, if ignoble, motivations; manipulated their elaborate plots in order to make their heroes' mistakes completely reasonable; ventilated the heroines' sufferings (and sometimes consolations) in detail. Their characters, good and bad alike, underwent sudden changes of heart or experienced overdue remorse in time to bring about the happy endings. To each of these writers, in short, slander was merely one element of an intricate story about psychologically interesting characters.

But Shakespeare chose not to work in this realistic vein as he dramatized the plight of the slandered woman for the first time. He made the characters lifelike, certainly, but he did not give them great depth. Much of Ariosto's psychology he tossed away: analyses of motives, presentations of internal debates, descriptions of shifting sentiments. He pared down the plot to its essentials of false accusation, discovery, and vindication, discarding the complicated machinery by which it had been executed in the other works. For what Shakespeare was emphasizing most was not the mechanism of the trap or the feelings of those caught in it, but something else: what slander is. Out of the source material he extracted the ethical issues, bringing to the center of his play the old sense—Gower's and Spenser's—of the absolute, devilish evil in calumny. The main plot of *Much Ado* belongs definitely in the tradition we have surveyed.[2]

An Elizabethan play to which this tradition is also central, Thomas Garter's *Susanna* (printed in 1578),[3] provides a most enlightening comparison with *Much Ado*. Garter's interlude is based on the Apocryphal narrative of Susanna and the Elders, the archetype of the story of the slandered and vindicated heroine.[4] *Much Ado* and *Susanna*, as Madeleine Doran has pointed out, are "in the same tradition of the romantic tale of trials successfully overpassed."[5] The Susanna story has strong lines, and Garter emphasizes them. His design is to bring out the stark oppositions inherent in the story; his disposition of moral opposites against one another resembles the medieval allegorists' arrangement of virtues against vices. Garter announces the play's aesthetic pattern: " . . . ofte the paynter in his workes, to show the fayrer whyte, / Doth set the blackest black of all, agaynst it ouer right" (825-26). The moral atmosphere of the play is unambiguous and the ethical poles are absolute; Garter is pointing to the nature of calumniation and the seriousness of its consequences. The false accusation flows from pure malice; the heroine's blamelessness is just as complete. As had the allegorists, Garter stresses the power of slander against innocence, expresses the old sense that honor is necessary to life itself, equates calumniation with death, sets faith and charity against suspicion and hate. Enveloping the play is the idea that slander is a peculiar kind of evil, not just another instance of man's normal inhumanity to man. It comes from a mysteriously satanic corner of the human heart, Garter suggests, and is so dangerous that recovery from its effects is a miracle.

If we set *Susanna* and *Much Ado* against the actual sources and analogues of the Hero-Claudio plot, we can better appreciate the logic of Shakespeare's treatment. The resemblances between the two plays are really striking. First, unlike the analogues of *Much Ado*, both *Susanna* and Shakespeare's play present largely unmotivated villains. The spite of Don John is like Gower's Envy and the "cancred malice" of Spenser's Slander, and it is also analogous to the "auncient spyght" which Garter's Satan feels. Secondly, Shakespeare leaves out a dramatic incident which appears in all the analogues; when he omits the window-scene he is emphasizing, as Garter does, the efficiency and force of slander. Thirdly, Shakespeare's version is the only one in which the innocent heroine is made to stand trial, confronted with the slander directly, and called upon to defend herself; again, a like scene appears in *Susanna*, polarizing goodness and evil. Fourthly, Shakespeare points up the necessity of publicizing the truth about Hero in the dénouement in a way which is similar to Garter's use of True Report, faith and love opposing envy as in Gower and Spenser. Fifthly, Shakespeare's choice of Dogberry and Verges as instruments of discovery is unprecedented in the analogues, where manipulation of plot or character provides the key to the truth. In the two plays, it is a providential force—a miracle—which rescues the heroine from infamy rather than, as in Ariosto and his followers, the progression of events or changes of heart. *Much Ado about Nothing*, with the old sense of the satanic nature of calumny behind it, brings out the strong lines submerged in its source material.

Shakespeare's most radical departure from Ariosto and his successors is his unmotivated villain. The change is a profound one. In all the other versions of the story except Spenser's (the story of Phedon in Book II of *The Faerie Queene*), a rival lover sets the plot into motion. The villain in the *Orlando Furioso* unsuccessfully woos the heroine; finally, his unrequited passion turned to hate, he determines to get revenge by staining her good name. Bandello's villain likewise acts from disappointed love; and although Beverley rhetorically attributes the trouble in his story to "that Serpent vile," "that treason black"[6] in the heart of his villain, his slanderer actually hopes to gain the lady for himself. Similar feelings impel the antagonist in Whetstone. The authors of all these stories give their villains the psychologically credible motivation of spurned love; and if this sort of resentment is ignoble, it is at least understandable. When Shakespeare deprives Don John of this motive without supplying another equally credible, he makes a new point: that slander springs from a purer malice. Don John's impulse is that of Envy as traditionally defined—arbitrary, absolute, mysterious. His wish to ruin Hero comes from nothing more, or less, than stark hatred of human goodness.[7] This villain suggests, says Bernard Spivack, "the theme of anti-love stitched in dark contrast . . . upon the bright fabric of love, the theme of sullen negation matched against a society of love and courtesy. . . . "[8]

If we have in mind the historical conception of Envy as we turn to Don John's characterization, the details suddenly look familiar. The other major characters in the play think, with Leonato, that it is much better "to weep at joy than to joy at weeping" (I.i.27-28). Don John not only takes pleasure in others' grief but also attributes his own ill will to generous people (" . . . their cheer is the greater that I am subdued. Would the cook were of my mind!"[9] [I.iii.74-75]). Don John's False Seeming is obvious: despite claims that he is "plain-dealing" rather than "flattering," he *is* a hypocrite—he *does* hide what he is (I.iii.32-34,14). Bringing his lies about Hero to Don Pedro he says, "You may think I love you not: let that appear hereafter, and aim better at me by that I now will manifest" (III.ii.97-99). The difference between this villain and the rejected lovers in the analogues of *Much Ado* is clear from his apologia (I.iii.11-19), where he admits to a "mortifying mischief." We never know exactly what the "occasion that breeds" (I.iii.4-5) his discontent is. His brother has forgiven him; he resents such graciousness. He does lament that Claudio "hath all the glory of my overthrow" (I.iii.68-69), but this sounds like a handy pretext, offered as it is after Don John has found out that a wedding is being planned which can serve for a "model to build mischief on" (I.iii.49); besides, resentment of another's success is traditionally an aspect of Envy. Shakespeare suggests a simplicity of motive when his villain says about

41

his discontent, "I make all use of it, for I use it only" (I.iii.41); when he explains, "Only to despite them, I will endeavour any thing" (II.i.31-32). Spenser had written that Envy's nature is to

> grudge at all,
> That euer she sees doen prays-worthily,
> Whose sight to her is greatest crosse. . . .
>
> (V.xii.31)

We are reminded of this and of the tradition behind it when Shakespeare's first slanderer says of Claudio, "If I can cross him any way, I bless myself every way" (I.iii.67-68); and again, "Any bar, any cross, any impediment will be medicinable to me" (II.ii.3-4). Finally, the imagery in Don John's self-portrait echoes older descriptions of envy and slander: "I had rather be a canker in a hedge than a rose in his grace, and it better fits my blood to be disdained of all than to fashion a carriage to rob love from any" (I.iii.28-32). We think of Gower's rose and nettle, the "cancred malice" of Spenser's slander. The contrasts in Don John's statement express his cynicism; his sullen nature aligns itself against the positive values of the play, love and generosity. Hero and Claudio become convenient victims of a generally envious spirit, one whose chosen weapon against the accord "q'est fait de bon amour"[10] is detraction.

Shakespeare, then, refused to use for his villain the psychological rationale supplied by his sources. He selected instead the method of characterizing Don John which would best emphasize the theme of the evil of slander. In this his strategy is like Garter's. The villain in *Susanna* is the Devil himself, who wants to destroy the most virtuous person in Israel to "see if God with all his myght, / Can defende this soule from our auncient spyght" (115-16). Obviously, his only motivation is his own nature; his weapon is slander, an allegorical character named Ill Report (the Vice in the play) that he has trained. In both *Much Ado* and *Susanna* the contrasts between malice and innocence, evil and good, remind us of the allegorical background. Don John's desire to destroy innocence and love, different in kind from the vengefulness felt by his counterparts in the analogues, is as enigmatic and outrageous as Satan's grudge against mankind.[11]

Shakespeare made another major change in his source material when he omitted the window-scene. As Bullough says, "It is truly remarkable that Shakespeare does not present the scene in which the hero sees his 'rival' climbing to his betrothed's window; for such a scene is found in all the analogues."[12] Ariosto and the others used the window-scene because of either its narrative value or its usefulness in explaining characters' thoughts and feelings, or both. They directed much attention to the strategems by which the villains "prove" their cases against the heroines. Because each of the heroes "sees" his beloved betraying him, his credulity makes sense. In Ariosto, for example, the maid explains how closely she resembled her mistress during the window incident prepared by the villain for the hero to watch. She had been tricked into dressing in the heroine's clothes and into receiving her own lover at the window "in all their sight." Ariosto emphasizes that the interpretation of the hero and his brother was the only reasonable one: " . . . we have plainly seene with both our eys, / Her filthie fact appeare without collusion."[13] The other authors who borrowed from Ariosto also emphasize the good quality of the evidence, making the reader see the situation through their heroes' eyes, enter into their feelings, and understand their judgments. Shakespeare's Claudio jumps so much more lightly to distrust of his beloved that many a reader of the play has refused to forgive him.

But Shakespeare took the excuses away from Claudio for a definite reason. Bullough suggests that he "refused to use [the window-scene] in order to draw attention to his major theme of hearsay and false report."[14] When he left out the "proof" of Hero's unchastity, Shakespeare pointed to the power of the unadorned lie. This sense that a false accusation *by itself* can destroy good name again aligns *Much Ado* with the allegorical tradition and *Susanna*. Both Garter and Shakespeare stress the idea that words can do irreparable damage, bringing out the quality in slander which Gower had identified as Malbouche, Detraction's chamberlain. The whole point about slander is that it works without evidence. If Malbouche "knows evil of people, he recites it, and if he does not know any he speaks the evil within himself" (*Mirour*, 2746-48). Shakespeare produces the effect of the power and efficiency of lies by omitting the ocular trickery which had deceived Claudio's counterparts. The accusation against Hero works much more like the calumniation Susanna suffers.

In Garter's play, the character Ill Report (who fits closely the traditional definition of slander) has been sent by his creator, Satan, to urge the Elders to tempt Susanna. Ill Report has been trained to talk in such a way

> That were she neuer so iust or true,
> Or liuer neuer so chast,
> By hooke, or crooke, by trace or pace,
> He bringes her home at last.   (47-50)

Ill Report notes that in him lies Satan's last hope of ruining the heroine.

Since Susanna is virtuous, only slander can destroy her good name. He announces that "... though the Deuill himselfe, could not tempt Susans grace / The wit of Mayster *Ill Report* hath her and it defaste" (183-84). This boast echoes Gower's statement that Detraction is more powerful against the virtuous than the Devil is (*Mirour*, 3790-92). Ill Report is the last and most dangerous weapon in Satan's arsenal. Garter exploits the idea that the goodness of Susanna's character will be no protection against the inventions of slander, "a maruailous force" (750). Until the discovery, the accusations that the Elders make up out of whole cloth ruin her honor just as effectively as publication of an actual crime would have done, so powerful is Ill Report's falsehood. Garter points to the unique power of detraction, as Shakespeare does, by stressing the fact that a simple lie nearly destroys a human life. These plays, in substituting talk for visual deception, make us think less about how slander operates than about exactly what it is.[15]

Shakespeare creates a scene for Hero and Claudio which is unprecedented in his sources and analogues. It boldly polarizes falseness against truth and malice against innocence, pointing up the theme of good fame. Claudio savagely denounces his betrothed not just in public, but at the altar on their wedding day.[16] Ariosto does not show his heroine confronted with the false accusation; Bandello's heroine, Fenicia, finds out through a messenger that her engagement has been called off. She is at home with her family when they receive word that her betrothed, Sir Timbreo, "does not mean to have you for his relatives ... because he has seen with his own eyes something in Fenicia that he would never have credited." To Fenicia he "says that the love which he bore you did not deserve the bitter reward you have given him, and that you should find yourself another husband, just as you have already found yourself another lover."[17] This accusation comes to Bandello's heroine in privacy; and although it is direct, the language of the message is courteous. We should compare the tone of Claudio's public denunciation: "There, Leonato, take her back again: / Give not this rotten orange to your friend" (IV.i.32-33). While contrasting strongly with treatments in the sources, Shakespeare's scene is similar to the one in which Susanna has to stand trial against Ill Report and the Elders. Both Hero and Susanna stand accused in public, helpless to reply to open slander. Garter and Shakespeare underline the brutality of detraction and dramatize its power over the innocent. On the witness stand Ill Report cries out Susanna's supposed shame: "A whore, yea vyle and fylthye whore, fye on it fylthy acte, / I thinke a thousand of her toyes, the vyldest whore doth lack" (795-96). Susanna is forced to unveil on the stand so that all can see her shame; she says,

44

Doe not I feele ynough good Lord, but all the world must see,
I mourne the lesse, O Lord thou knowest an innocent to dye,
But yet my greefe is to to great, to end with infamy.

(1002-04)

Shakespeare achieves the same ugly effect in Claudio's statements about
Hero's seeming modesty (IV.i.34-42). The dramatist captures the essence of
the menace in calumny with Claudio's accusation that even Hero's blush is
feigned: "O, what authority and show of truth / Can cunning sin cover itself
withal!" (IV.i.36-37) Both Susanna and Hero suffer the humiliation of
public exposure.

And it is because both playwrights are accentuating the moral seriousness
of slander and the meaning of defamation that their accused women are
passive and helpless in these scenes. Bandello's Fenicia is very different. She
talks about her situation at great length to the many "gentle ladies, relatives,
and friends" who come to console her. She answers the accusation, affirming
her innocence to these sympathizers and finding comfort in their knowledge
of the truth. She decides that the grief and pain of being slandered are not
important in the scheme of things: "It is enough for me that before the just
tribunal of Christ I shall be known innocent of such baseness" (p. 120). But
Garter and Shakespeare stress the ethical content of the situation with their
quiet heroines. Hero's behavior fits her role in the story. She does not deny
Claudio's accusation; she is bewildered and incredulous, able only to cry for
help: "O, God defend me! How am I beset! / What kind of catechising call
you this?" (IV.i.78-79) When pressed she can say only, "I talk'd with no
man at that hour, my lord" (IV.i.87). Susanna likewise fails to counteract
the charge against her. When told, "Speake for thy selfe it is high tyme"
(1040) she gives up instead: "Behold my God I dye therefore, through
mallice of their harte, / Therefore my God receaue my soule, none else can
ease my smarte" (1049-50). These accused women behave in accordance
with the traditional sense that the victim of detraction is helpless.

We find in both *Susanna* and *Much Ado* much emphasis on the absolute
necessity that the unjustly accused woman regain her good fame, that the
truth be widely publicized. This is not so in the "realistic" versions of Hero's
story. In connection with the "rebirths" of the heroines both Garter and
Shakespeare point emphatically to the old association of good name with life
itself and also set against slander, and the trouble it brings, the love and
faith which counteract it.

Susanna's father expresses the idea that society's good opinion of a person

45

is as important as that person's very life. At a point before the truth comes out, he prays:

> And therefore Lord if our offence, or else her owne desarte,
> Haue bene the cause of this her fall, yet quallify her smarte,
> And graunt that with her lyfe, her fame may also dye,
> And that we heare no more her fault, this onely bowne aske I.

$$(862-65)$$

Shakespeare expresses the same idea through the Friar, who predicts that "The supposition of the lady's death / Will quench the wonder of her infamy" (IV.i.239-40). In fact, one artistic purpose of Hero's apparent death is to underline the identity of good name with life itself. This is not the case with the parallel incident in Bandello. The slandered Fenicia's father announces that she is dead and raises a pretended epitaph which attributes her death to slander (p. 122). But as Prouty points out, the reason for the pretended death is practical.[18] The father sends Fenicia away secretly, hoping that after her appearance has changed "as is usual with age, he might marry her off in two or three years under another name" (p. 122). Hero's "death" has an entirely different purpose. The Friar imagines that the news of it will make Claudio regret having accused her, but says that a more important effect will be the restoration of her good name:

> Marry, this well carried shall on her behalf
> Change slander to remorse; that is some good:
> But not for that dream I on this strange course,
> But on this travail look for greater birth.

$$(IV.i.212-15)$$

"Come, lady, die to live" (IV.i.255) completes the equation between life and reputation.[19]

In each of these plays careful oppositions between the maliciousness of slander and belief in the purity of the heroine, the envious spirit and love, remind us of the allegorical definition of slander. In *Susanna*, a character named True Report and one of Susanna's servants are on stage to express belief in her goodness. Their function is analogous to that of Beatrice and Benedick after the denunciation scene. Even though True Report's part is not nearly so large as that of the Vice, the contrast between the two characters is structurally important, providing the suggestion that the spirit of charity and faith is needed to overcome slander. The servant in *Susanna* is immediately suspicious about the disclosure of the Elders after the orchard scene, and tells True Report so. True Report agrees that the Elders' accusations must be false:

> Our Mistresse, yea she doth her lyfe, in such sorte still direct,
> As fyckle fame at no tyme durst, her honest lyfe suspect,
> I tell thee true Seruus my friend, I flatter not for meede,
> It shalbe found that they them selues haue wrought
>   this wicked deede.   (787-90)

This exchange has a parallel in Beatrice's equally immediate reaction, "O, on my soul, my cousin is belied!" (IV.i.148) and Benedick's guess that the practice of the deception "lives in John the bastard, / Whose spirits toil in frame of villanies" (IV.i.190-91). The element of belief in the heroine's goodness receives emphasis in both plays, good will finally emerging as a powerful warrior against slander.

The method of discovery Shakespeare chooses is radically different from those used by Ariosto and the other "realistic" writers. Again, it is formally very like Garter's. Ariosto solves his heroine's problem by making the maid sorry about her participation in the slander scheme and anxious to justify herself. She tells the whole story to the wandering hero. In Bandello, regretful feelings on the part of the basically honorable villain bring about the discovery, as he volunteers the whole story to the hero. A change of heart likewise motivates the hero of Beverley's story to fight for the honor of the slandered lady: "Record of former amitie, forgettes supposd offence."[20] Garter and Shakespeare do not attempt to achieve the discovery either through the logical sequence of events or through the logic of character, but instead suggest a force outside the story working against the slander, more or less inevitably to help the accused woman overcome her trials.

In *Susanna*, as in miracle plays and *sacre rappresentazioni* on the subject of the slandered heroine, the discovery is a miracle.[21] "God rayseth the spirite of Danyell" to ask those taken in by Ill Report, " . . . are you fooles O Israell, or are your wits dismayde. / Or haue you not the pollicie, the truth to know and trie" (1068-69). Garter states that God has given Israel a warning by Daniel (1179-84), who shows the Elders that slander has rebounded to entrap them: " . . . thy tongue hath thee betrayde" (1187). Shakespeare's mechanism of discovery may not be very different in kind; is the effectiveness of the Watch an accident, a miracle, or both? Borachio is very quickly disarmed when Don Pedro questions him in front of the Watch and his confession is swift and full (V.i.236-51). He says, "I have deceived even your very eyes" in a spirit not of boastfulness but of shame; and his estimate, "What your wisdoms could not discover, these shallow fools have brought to light" does not reflect adversely on the princes so much as point to the providential inevitability of the discovery. Likewise Daniel says to Susanna's judges, "Go sit in iudgement once agayne, the witness they haue borne, / Is false, and yet their grauity, your sences doth subborne" (1073-74). Borachio's repentance is not necessary for the discovery as the regrets of Ariosto's maid and Bandello's villain are, because we have seen the Watch on the verge of making the revelation and know that it will come. Shakespeare has prepared for this scene by the introduction of Dogberry and Verges before the ceremony and has created suspense out of their ineptness. But nevertheless Dogberry and Verges have given the impression that they could not have better hid the information had they tried, and its revelation is either a miraculous accident or an uproarious miracle. The strange overturning of expectation which brings out truth is common only to Garter and Shakespeare; it suggests good winning out over evil in a providential rather than practical way. That a transcendent force unravels the mysterious wrong of calumny in these plays is in keeping with the traditional conception of slander—for if malicious utterance against a person's good name is a "maruailous force," nothing less than another supernatural power can overcome it.[22]

A final comparison can illustrate the difference in feeling and emphasis between the "realistic" slander stories and these two plays. The scene in which Claudio marries Hero's "sister" has a precise counterpart in Bandello. Bandello's ceremony satisfies the impulses of generous sentiment. The reader's suspense stems from waiting while the hero first laments having caused the loss of his first bride and then realizes that the new one is his very Fenicia. Finally recognizing his beloved, the hero was "filled with infinite joy and gazing on her endlessly . . . and all the time he wept gently, unable to form words but telling himself that he had been blind" (p. 130). Shakespeare gives the recognition scene an entirely different point. As his heroine unmasks, he makes us contemplate how literally her adventure has been a matter of life and death:

> Claud. Another Hero!
> Hero.   Nothing certainer:
> One Hero died defiled, but I do live,
> And surely as I live, I am a maid.
> D. Pedro. The former Hero! Hero that is dead!
> Leon. She died, my Lord, but whiles her slander lived.
>
> (V.iv.62-66)

This is the new birth which the Friar predicted; the sense that Hero could

48

not have lived with the slander is clear. In a remarkable parallel, Susanna prays, grateful to God for having vindicated her:

> No, no, good Lord aboue the rest, to prayse thee I am bound,
> That me doest helpe myraculously, and eake my foes confound.
> I was but dead, and thou to lyfe, restoredst me silly wight.

(1427-29)

Celebration of a "rebirth" in these plays is proportionate to the deadliness of the danger overcome. "Maruaylous," Ill Report had said, is "The pollicy of the Deuill, the enuie he doth beare, / The man he seekes to ouerthrow, all such as God doth feare" (147-49).

Shakespeare's responses to his material were very different from those of Beverley and Whetstone, as Prouty said.[23] Shakespeare saw into the heart of the story; he simplified characterization so as to concentrate on the theme of devilish slander and providential rescue. The bold artistic scheme of the Hero-Claudio plot is in harmony with the tradition exemplified by Gower, Spenser, and Garter.[24] Garter's Devil and his Vice help to elucidate Shakespeare's first slanderer—and point toward his next: Iago.

CHAPTER THREE

Villainy in *Othello*:
Shakespeare's Anatomy of Envy

One speculates that Don John, Hero, and Claudio stuck in their creator's mind. The envious villain, the slandered bride, the credulous groom: Shakespeare had sketched them quickly for his busy comedy of "Benedicte and Betteris," using just enough detail to bring them to life and engage our interest in their story. Now he imagined these characters again, as principals of a tragedy.

While he had suppressed the psychological element in fashioning *Much Ado* from its sources, Shakespeare now reversed the process, giving Cinthio's flat characters supreme individuality. In the Italian tale of "Disdemona," "the Moor," and "the Ensign," there was little psychological analysis. Shakespeare gave these characters inner lives, deepening them immeasurably. On his stage Cinthio's conventional figures became intensely, agonizingly real.

But the alterations which produced Iago were perhaps the most profound. Like Don John's counterparts in Ariosto and Bandello, Cinthio's slanderer acted out of disappointed passion. The Ensign, handsome but wicked, "fell ardently in love with Disdemona, and bent all his thoughts to see if he could enjoy her." But she, "whose every thought was for the Moor," did not even notice his overtures. He began to imagine that "this was because she was in love with the Corporal; and he wondered how he might remove the latter from her sight. Not only did he turn his mind to this, but the love which he had felt for the Lady now changed to the bitterest hate, and he gave himself up to studying how to bring it about that, once the Corporal were killed, if he himself could not enjoy the Lady, then the Moor should not have her either."[1] Presented with this motive a second time, Shakespeare again refused to use it. Again he substituted for embittered love a more complicated set of impulses and purposes, a more fundamental evil. Iago descends not so much from Cinthio's Ensign as from Shakespeare's own first slanderer (and the tradition behind him). Having suggested in Don John that it is a malice like Satan's which most characteristically strikes at the happiness of others through lies, Shakespeare went on in Iago to anatomize this malice. Although dissimilar in treatment, the two villains are of a kind. And, from one point of view, at least, they are as different from their prototypes as they could possibly be. For the motive which Shakespeare selected for them is, instead of love turned to hatred, a hate that not only has never been love, but has never been anything else at all.

This motive, which Iago acknowledges to Roderigo at the beginning of the play and repeatedly thereafter, underlies the rest: "I have told thee often, and I retell thee again and again, I hate the Moor: my cause is hearted" (I.iii.372-74). The lines recall John's Epistle ("He who hates his brother walks in darkness...") and St. Cyprian on envy ("...it is a calamity without a remedy to hate one who is happy").[2] As the man on Shakespeare's stage reiterates the theme, we realize that his enmity has a hollow quality. Gower had called on the envious person to account for his hatred of his friend, held "without cause and with pleasure": "Answer this, why do you do such evil?"[3] There is no explanation. In *Nature* Envy, boasting of having destroyed Pride, is asked, "What moveth thee thereto?" He answers,

> Marry! cause had I none;
> But only that it is my guise
> When I see another man arise,
> Or fare better than I,
> Then must I chafe and fret for ire,
> And imagine, with all my desire,
> To destroy him utterly.[4]

When Othello asks the officials to

> demand that demi-devil
> Why he hath thus ensnared my soul and body,
>
> (V.ii.300-01)

Iago will refuse to answer. His malice is just itself, like Archimago's hostility toward Una.

The general nature of Iago's malevolence has long been recognized. His devilishness is obvious; the nature of his relationship to the Father of Lies has been the subject of much debate.[5] But if we place him against the background we have surveyed, the integrity and artistry of his characterization become more strikingly apparent. Although, because he is so human, he is a puzzle we never quite solve, we can fit some of the pieces together better by referring to a model like this one (from Gower's *Mirour*) of the Sin most like Satan himself:

> These are the offices of Envy:
> First, to speak ill of her neighbor,

51

Then to enjoy the ills of others
And grieve over her neighbors' prosperity.
To supplant them she devotes pains and efforts;
And by a feigned and false seeming
She becomes privy to others' counsels
And then makes them known.
Then in the end she causes the dishonor
Of these men and women
Whose hearty friend she has become.

(*Mirour*, 3697-708)

This definition illuminates a character whose envy (in a less "technical," usually a more modern sense) has already been much discussed. The pieces interlock, but can be separated for the purpose of discussion: Iago's grief and his mirth, his hypocrisy, his lying, and his ambition.

Othello's tormentor does have emotions—the sorrows and joys of Envy. Always making comparisons, Envy is grieved by another's honor, beauty, health, joy; to her many real sorrows, she adds imagined ones. Violent-hearted Dissension always follows her (*Mirour*, 3061). Iago resolves that Cassio must die not only because he represents a threat, but because

He hath a daily beauty in his life
That makes me ugly.... (V.i.20-21)

The villain grieves over Othello's happiness with Desdemona, perfect at the beginning of the play. To recognize Othello's "constant, loving, noble," "free and open nature" (II.i.298; I.iii.405) is painful enough; now in addition the envier must contemplate his "full fortune" (I.i.66). In traditional language he speaks of spoiling it as he instructs Roderigo:

make after him, poison his delight,
. . .
And, though he in a fertile climate dwell,
Plague him with flies: though that his joy be joy,
Yet throw such changes of vexation on't,
As it may lose some colour. (I.i.68-73)

No blessing, worldly or spiritual, is too small or too great to sadden the envious. Gower's "Dolour" had lost her appetite on finding someone in a higher place at the dinner table, had sorrowed because others rejoiced in the promise of the Resurrection (*Mirour*, 3037-39; 3114-20). Iago finds food for his bitterness everywhere, but nothing pains him more sharply than Othello's joy.

The other side of this sorrow is the "gladschipe of Envie," as Gower calls it in the *Confessio.* Iago's jocularity, so heartfelt that Spivack views it as "the true passion of the tragic agent throughout this play,"[6] connects him with the Vice; but it is also one of the "offices of Envy." The invidious are gladdened by any kind of trouble-making, but especially by slander. The sin in the *Mirour* presides with satisfaction over someone's decline: "See! / What he attained 'du mal engin,' / He lost deservedly" (*Mirour*, 3172-74). So Iago interprets for Lodovico the jealous Moor's ugly and violent behavior: "He is much changed" (IV.i.279). Seeing a man fall from prosperity and honor, envious joy "raises a common clamor" in order to abase him further (*Mirour*, 3183-85). When Malbouche spreads his lies, she cannot keep from laughing (*Mirour*, 3221). Iago's "gaiety in destruction"[7] ranges from simple pleasure —"sport"—to intricate irony, the more delectable to him because he is the only one on the stage who can appreciate it. "If thou canst cuckold him," he tells Roderigo, "thou dost thyself a pleasure, me a sport" (I.iii.376-77). He uses his gull for "sport and profit" (I.iii.392). The night which he spends ruining Cassio proves that "Pleasure and action make the hours seem short" (II.iii.384). The pleasure is "Joye d'autry mal"; the refrain, the "special song of Envy" (*Mirour*, 3166). On one level, the ills of Cassio and Othello are simply entertainment.

But the entertainment is also much more sophisticated, as this "precious villain" (V.ii.235) savors the irony which stems from his role as its secret author. In his mind the entire action, "here, but yet confused" early in Act Two (i.320), is a kind of joke on Othello. After relating several of his famous "proximate motives"[8]—lust for Desdemona, suspicion of both Othello and Cassio with his own wife—Iago arrives at a formulation of the joke. It reveals the primary motive, a profound envious "gladschipe." Iago will

> Make the Moor thank me, love me and reward me,
> For making him egregiously an ass
> And practising upon his peace and quiet
> Even to madness.   (II.i.317-20)

This expresses a relish much rarer than delight in others' griefs. What the villain anticipates with most intense enjoyment is the irony at the heart of the tragedy: that Othello will come to meet, even embrace, his trouble. This is Iago's private "joke." Not only will no one else in the play understand it, but no one except Roderigo will even be aware that it is being perpetrated. The whole plot is hidden, of course, by False Seeming.

False Seeming, to return to our most precise definition, is not merely dissimulation (which is one of its subdivisions), it is pretended love;

False Seeming's beautiful face
Is horrible yet seems cheerful
Thinking ill she speaks fair words
Makes what is sweet bitter,
And having turned her back
Makes white change into black.
Her ointment is so stinging,
That her kiss kills with mortal venom
And behind her tears the traitor laughs.

(Mirour, 3493-501)

Envy masquerades as love, its opposite. Iago announces at the beginning that his face belies his heart, that he is one of those "Who, trimm'd in forms and visages of duty, / Keep yet their hearts attending on themselves":

Heaven is my judge, not I for love and duty,
But seeming so, for my peculiar end. . . .

(I.i.50-51, 59-60)

He sets forth the ancient antithesis:

Though I do hate him as I do hell-pains,
. . .
I must show out a flag and sign of love,
Which is indeed but sign.   (I.i.155-58)

Iago knows what truthful people like Othello take to be the purpose of signs (and words); he knows that, thinking "men honest that but seem to be so" (I.iii.406), the others will accept him at face value. Again and again he swears by his love for the two men whose destruction he is engineering; False Seeming, in the allegorists, had been epitomized by Judas' kiss. Having drawn Cassio into drunkenness and then slandered him,[9] the hawk puts on pheasant's feathers (*Mirour,* 3502):

I do love Cassio well; and would do much
To cure him of this evil. . . .   (II.iii.148-49)

When charged (on his love and as a soldier) to explain the uproar and "mutiny" that he has staged, Iago creates the illusion that his love for Cassio and his honesty are in conflict. He does what one in such a situation might naturally do, speaks the "truth" but casts about for ways to explain Cassio's unjustifiable conduct. Here however, as he intends, imagination fails, and the testimony ends with an excuse so weak that it is damning:

54

> Yet surely Cassio, I believe, received
> From him that fled some strange indignity,
> Which patience could not pass.   (II.iii.244-46)

Othello "sees through" Iago's attempt to defend his friend, and the credibility of the disguise has been enhanced:

> I know, Iago
> Thy honesty and love doth mince this matter,
> Making it light to Cassio.   (II.iii.247-49)

And it is "love and honesty" which Othello must penetrate in the temptation scene in order to find out Iago's monstrous secret: "if thou dost love me," the hero says, "Show me thy thought" (III.iii.115-16). Again Iago seems to perceive a duty divided between friendship and truth; the well-wisher would like to protect Othello from harmful knowledge. Having planted the first seeds of suspicion, he asks to be excused from revealing his "uncleanly apprehensions" (III.iii.139) about Cassio. It is Othello who insists:

> Thou dost conspire against thy friend, Iago,
> If thou but think'st him wrong'd and makest his ear
> A stranger to thy thoughts.   (III.iii.142-44)

This should resolve the dilemma: Iago as a friend must tell what he knows. Thus the slanderer arranges that Othello, pursuing the fabrication, "[build himself] a trouble" (II.iii.150). Suggesting ever more strongly that his hidden knowledge would endanger Othello's "quiet," the loyal friend still refuses to yield it up:

> *Oth.*   By heaven I'll know thy thoughts.
> *Iago.*   You cannot, if my heart were in your hand.
>
>   (III.iii.162-63)

But now he warns against jealousy, and when Othello answers that he is not easily jealous, Iago takes his cue:

> I am glad of it; for now I shall have reason
> To show the love and duty that I bear you
> With franker spirit. . . .   (III.iii.193-95)

The scorpion stings; within a few lines Desdemona's truth has become "seeming" (III.iii.209). The "friend" apologizes for his candor:

> *Iago.*   I humbly do beseech you of your pardon
> For too much loving you.
> *Oth.*   I am bound to thee for ever.   (III.iii.212-13)

Later, while they are discussing proof, Othello is on the verge of recognition. He warns his deceiver, "If thou dost slander her and torture me, / Never pray more; abandon all remorse ..." (III.iii.368-69). Alerted to danger, hate rearranges its mask:

> O monstrous world!   Take note, take note, O world,
> To be direct and honest is not safe.
> Thank you for this profit; and from hence
> I'll love no friend, sith love breeds such offence.

> (III.iii.377-80)

The fair words of False Seeming, the scorpion with the friendly face, are brilliantly chosen. Pausing only momentarily to wonder whether it is Desdemona or Iago who is honest, Othello resumes his pursuit of "knowledge," disquiet, and death.

The poison takes full effect. Othello describes how it has changed him:

> Look here, Iago;
> All my fond love thus do I blow to heaven.
> 'Tis gone.
> Arise, black vengeance, from thy hollow cell!
> Yield up, O love, thy crown and hearted throne
> To tyrannous hate!   Swell, bosom, with thy fraught,
> For 'tis of aspics' tongues!

> (III.iii.444-50)

The language suggests what "marvellous force" has so swiftly turned beauty, love and peace into their opposites. The lines are full of dramatic irony, as Othello points to the venom in his heart without knowing how it got there. His transformation and the tragedy as a whole are above all, of course, the work of slander. We watch Iago "[shape] faults that are not" (III.iii.148), shape them, moreover, out of exceptional virtues. Then we watch while his lies, incredibly, destroy a paradise.

As Shakespeare's most naturalistically conceived slanderer, Iago, although diabolic, is a recognizable human type. St. Basil, following Aristotle, had pointed to the skill of the envious in "making what is praiseworthy seem despicable by means of unflattering distortions and in slandering virtue through the vice that is neighbor to it."[10] Not having ideals and perhaps not understanding them, he gives every good thing an ugly name. Love is sensuality only, one of our "carnal stings" (I.iii.336). The marriage contract is a "frail vow" (I.iii.362). Desdemona loved Othello not for his history, his "honours and his valiant parts" (I.iii.254), but for "bragging and telling her

56

fantasticall lies" (II.i.225). Cassio's "excellent courtesy" (II.i.177) is merely a "seeming" which cloaks lechery, as Desdemona's courtesy is really lust.

Whether or not Iago actually believes these things (for he tells them to Roderigo), he will make what is praiseworthy—Cassio's honesty, Desdemona's generosity—seem despicable to Othello. The plot succeeds because the slanderer can depend upon his victims to be themselves; they remain the same while he improvises; he sets the trap where he knows they will walk.[11] Desdemona will do everything she can to bind the broken joint between Cassio and her husband, and while she does,

> I'll pour this pestilence into his ear,
> That she repeals him for her body's lust;
> And by how much she strives to do him good,
> She shall undo her credit with the Moor.

The plan is perfect in its economy:

> So will I turn her virtue into pitch,
> And out of her own goodness make the net
> That shall enmesh them all.   (II.iii.362-68)

It works because they are all good. Cassio and Desdemona behave exactly as he knows they will, and Othello, being himself too, does not see through Iago's matchless falsity. So they all walk into the trap, and it springs; "Her name, that was as fresh / As Dian's visage, is now begrimed and black ... " (III.iii.386-87). Cassio's death is planned, and Iago is promoted. Othello's passion becomes his "instruction" (IV.i.41); he is fallen. Iago says:

> My medicine, work!   Thus credulous fools are caught;
> And many worthy and chaste dames even thus,
> All guiltless, meet reproach.   (IV.i.46-48)

The medicine, the pestilence, has made goodness seem ugly and has actually transfigured Othello's heart.

In his moment of hesitation Othello ironically suggests the depth and nature of Iago's evil, directing our attention to the theme:

> If thou dost slander her and torture me,
> Never pray more; abandon all remorse;
> On horror's head horrors accumulate;
> Do deeds to make heaven weep, all earth amazed;
> For nothing canst thou to damnation add
> Greater than that.   (III.iii.368-73)

Bravely Emilia, like Beatrice and Benedick, Pisanio and Paulina, raises her voice against the slander. She points to the kind of evil that is in Othello's delusion:

> If any wretch have put this in your head,
> Let heaven requite it with the serpent's curse!

$$(IV.ii.15-16)$$

And she tries to imagine what kind of man would accuse Desdemona: "Some eternal villain, / Some busy and insinuating rogue, / Some cogging, cozening slave, to get some office . . . " (IV.ii.130-32). When she discovers the facts, the only term she can think of for Iago's evil is a generic one:

> Villany, villany, villany!
> I think upon't, I think: I smell't: O villany!—
> I thought so then:—I'll kill myself for grief:—
> O villany, villany!   (V.ii.190-93)

And to Othello, she points out what, in believing and repeating the slander, he has become:

> Thou dost belie her, and thou art a devil.

$$(V.ii.133)$$

Although the name is hyperbolic, Othello has followed one who is on the Devil's side, and his tragedy is greater than Desdemona's. Gower had written in the *Mirour*: "He who has committed the offense of slander / Is bound to the enemy / So that he cannot part from him / Unless rescued by a special grace" (*Mirour*, 2649-52).

Madeleine Doran points out that there is a most terrible irony in the destruction of Othello, Iago's primary victim. The play opens with the slanderer's first attempt to blemish Othello's reputation. "In the end, though he does not at the start see so far ahead, he will goad him to commit the crime which will seem to turn the lies to truth."[12] Cassio and Desdemona, completely blameless, are completely vindicated. But Othello's infamy is earned. Thus, even though Desdemona has died in dreadful grief, Iago's lies have done the most damage not to the people about whom they were told, but to the person who listened to them. Othello distinguishes himself from his persecutor—"For nought I did in hate, but all in honour" (V.ii.295)—but he acknowledges his guilt. This, the metamorphosis of the hero himself, is certainly Iago's masterpiece.

Having seen all this, the deep ill will and its "symptoms" in the villain of

Shakespeare's tragedy of slander, we must consider his ambition. Iago wants Cassio's place; after repeating, "I hate the Moor," he thinks of the lieutenant:

> Cassio's a proper man: let me see now:
> To get his place and to plume up my will
> In double knavery—How, how?—Let's see:—

(I.iii.398-400)

The "displanting of Cassio" (II.i.282), although it figures in Iago's motivation, is not especially important by itself. For ambition, we know, is another of Envy's traditional manifestations. Cyprian and Basil had treated invidiousness as an ill both spiritual and worldly; they wrote not only of the envier's hostility to God but of his tendency to resent success, Cyprian citing the man who "complains that he himself rather has not been ordained or disdains to tolerate another who has been placed over him."[13] Gower's Supplanting fastens on another's office, honor, goods, power; she devises the other's ill so that she may gain his possessions. Supplanting is attended by Ambition and Confusion, this last a hound following the healthy man, waiting for him to be cast down (*Mirour*, 3436-38).

So Iago's desire to get Cassio's place and his purer hatreds can be viewed as patches of the same cloth. But still, after Iago replaces Cassio, his "ambition is satisfied; his devilish love of mischief is not."[14] It is natural that Emilia thinks of the more ordinary motive, the one which is even socially acceptable in itself.[15] But she glimpses the deeper truth at the same time, mentions the root as well as the branch, hypothesizes both an "eternal villain" and a "cozening slave." We may not be able to say where Iago's interest in personal gain leaves off and his desire to torture Othello begins, but the two impulses are reconcilable enough.

When we have superimposed this stunningly realistic characterization on the old allegorical image, its coherence becomes more readily apparent. Iago's hostility—lacking, as Spivack says, an "objective correlative"[16]—is deliberately mysterious and inhuman. He is not the Devil, but he is following the Devil, through whose envy death came into the world. "What can be made out of the instigation that exists for Iago in Cassio's daily beauty, in the attractions of double knavery, and in his frequently voiced hatred of Othello?" Spivack asks.[17] The inherited definition of Envy, since it encompasses all these motives and Iago's methods also, provides an interesting, although certainly partial, answer. And as the vices subordinate to Envy had shaded off into one another and coalesced, so in Iago malevolence, slander, pretense and ambition interlace. He is an envious man, hiding in Othello's garden. We may agree that the "central subject of *Othello* is love, and jealousy, which is a disease of love."[18] The central conflict in the play, this analysis of Iago suggests, is between love and its traditional enemy, envy.

Iago's prototype in Cinthio, to recapitulate, had been moved to slander by a perfectly intelligible (even an ordinary) human impulse: rejected passion. For this Shakespeare substituted something outrageous, inhuman, enigmatic. And Cinthio's faceless villain became concretely, dazzlingly real. What Shakespeare had suggested in *Much Ado about Nothing*, he scrutinized in *Othello*; envy and slander took on such vitality that their success was inevitable. Seeing the play, we believe that Iago commits "the werst of all synnes." There can be no miraculous rescue; for, while the falsely accused heroine can be vindicated, the hero's innocence cannot be restored. Don John had led in his creator's mind to Iago, but with Iago the inquiry into Envy was closed. When Shakespeare wrote on the theme of slander again, he concentrated on the false utterance itself, finally detaching it from any question of motive entirely.

CHAPTER FOUR

Cymbeline:
Shakespeare's Wager Story

When he next returned to the theme of the slandered woman (after having written *King Lear, Timon of Athens, Macbeth, Antony and Cleopatra,* and *Coriolanus*), Shakespeare selected a plot in which motive is not especially significant. Typically the villain in the wager plot is initially "inspired by lust, or envy, or malice" toward a brother of the heroine to wager that he can seduce her.[1] But when later he slanders her, by falsely claiming success, it is in order to win the bet. The profit motive may be considered a rationalization of the purer malice that triggers the scheme against Susanna; the slanderer acts not out of spite but in order to win florins, ducats, or guilders. Shakespeare used the received motive for his third slanderer, but only to get the play started. Iachimo's villainy, a realistic blend of cynicism, malice, and cupidity, is dramatically adequate (and effective) but not important for its own sake. For now Shakespeare shifted his principal attention to the other side of the calumniated woman story, and "viperous slander" itself became his controlling theme.

Again, it was a theme subordinated to much else in the sources. The ninth novel of the second day in the *Decameron* (generally viewed as the primary model for *Cymbeline*) is a typical wager story. It begins as a group of Italian merchants, away from home on business, talk idly after dinner. They are casual husbands, certain that their wives also have "wit enought to make use of their time" when alone at home.[2] As they jest about the infidelity of women, one Bernardo is moved to defend his wife's excellence and chastity. He is laughingly challenged by Ambrogiuolo, who believes that all women are frail. Bernardo confidently proposes the wager and Ambrogiuolo accepts. The villain goes to Genoa, hears about the good fame of Bernardo's wife Genevra, and—quickly realizing that he can win the bet only by deceit— bribes a poor woman to have him carried in a chest into Genevra's bedroom. While the heroine sleeps he observes details of the room and a birthmark on her breast, and steals some of her belongings. Once back in Paris, he reports to Bernardo that he has won the wager, convincing him only with the revelation about the birthmark. The shattered hero pays up and leaves for home.

61

From the outskirts of Genoa he sends a servant into the city with instructions to kill Genevra while ostensibly escorting her to him. The servant intends to do as he is told, but Genevra, promising to leave the country, persuades him to spare her. She disguises herself as a sailor and after much travel gains employment in Alexandria as one of the Sultan's foremost "men." At an international fair she meets the villain and recognizes her own purse and girdle in his shop. As she questions him he tells her about the wager, boasting of having won it by seducing Bernardo's wife. Feigning friendship, she arranges a confrontation between him and Bernardo. The liar is forced to tell the story as it really happened; Genevra reveals her true identity and pardons Bernardo; on the Sultan's order the villain is tied to a stake, smeared with honey, and left in the sun to a death hastened by flies, wasps, and hornets: "the deceiver is trampled and trod, by such as himself hath deceived."[3] This worldly tale subordinates themes of honor and defamation to concentrate on the tangible; it achieves its resolution realistically. This pragmatic emphasis is characteristic of the wager type.

For *Cymbeline* Shakespeare probably drew on both Boccaccio's tale and another representative wager story, closely related geneologically to Boccaccio's, the English *Frederyke of Jennen*.[4] But among the more distant analogues of *Cymbeline* is a version which provides another reference point: a French miracle play with a wager plot. The *Miracle d'Oton, roi d'Espagne*[5] uses the gambling incident but retains the formal characteristics of the elemental slandered woman tale, emphasizing theme, underlining contrasting ethical absolutes, and resolving the woman's plight through miraculous intervention. In this version the villain (Berengier) attempts to win the wager legitimately by offering the heroine (Denise) his love. She rejects him indignantly, but he persuades her attendant to get the evidence which will seem to prove his success. An unnamed citizen hears of the wager and on his own initiative reveals the whole scheme to Denise; the Virgin Mary appears to tell her what to do. Her deluded husband, also helped by a vision from heaven, overtakes the traitor just in time to challenge and defeat him.

While this play, like the sources of *Cymbeline*, deviates from the basic slandered woman plot, it is nevertheless much closer than they are to the archetype; it systematically counterpoises ethical opposites, in accordance with the tradition we have scrutinized. And Shakespeare, once again working against the grain of an often told tale, reorders the wager material in the same way. Aesthetically *Cymbeline* belongs with the remote analogue rather than with those nearer to Shakespeare's hand. *Cymbeline* shares significant non-Boccaccian features with the French play: the villain's attempt on the heroine's honor; her knowledge of the false accusation; the presence and participation of a character like True Report; and an element which has bothered *Cymbeline* critics but which is made much more explicable through comparison with the religious play, the divine intervention which ends the woman's sufferings. Two other features of *Cymbeline*, departures from its probable sources and near analogues, serve to heighten the old conception of slander, "Whose edge is sharper than the sword" (III.iv.34): Shakespeare's fairy-tale setting and his handling of the wager scene.[6] Whatever wager stories Shakespeare actually knew and used as sources for this romance, he was again borrowing a quite realistic accused woman tale and treating it in another mode. The mercantile element prominent in the source material recedes; *Cymbeline* magnifies, through a somewhat clouded medium, the ancient sense that "viperous slander" (III.iv.41) is the ruin of love.

Shakespeare sets the wager plot within a more primitive type of persecution story. From Boccaccio's contemporary middle-class world we move to a legendary country: to a palace where the princess is imprisoned by the cruel king and the cruel stepmother, later to a cave in the mountains where she is rescued. This fairy-tale framework with its black and white characters, its deep contrasts, parallels and enhances the pattern of oppositions in Shakespeare's wager plot. By means of the frame story Shakespeare emphasizes the theme of the unjustly persecuted heroine and also points up the evil of the slander which arises from the wager. For as wicked as the tyrannical father and the homicidal queen are, they are not Imogen's worst enemies, because their viciousness is easily recognizable. When the queen protests, "No, be assured you shall not find me, daughter, / After the slander of most stepmothers, / Evil-eyed unto you" (I.i.70-72), she is merely labeling her already transparent falsity. When she pronounces her "pity" for the "pangs of barr'd affections," Imogen easily perceives that this is "Dissembling courtesy" (I.i.81-83). Nor is the persecuted heroine intimidated by Cymbeline's continual raging; she tells him, "I am senseless of your wrath; a touch more rare / Subdues all pangs, all fears" (I.i.135-36). With each scene that takes place at the palace we are shown that Imogen's enemies here, however cruel, are doomed to failure. The queen's plans to poison Pisanio, Posthumus' faithful servant, and then Imogen herself, will not materialize; for the doctor, suspicious, has given her harmless drugs:

> I do know her spirit,
> And will not trust one of her malice with
> A drug of such damn'd nature. (I.v.34-36)

The queen's promise of preferment will not bribe the faithful servant to betray the lovers: "... when to my good lord I prove untrue, / I'll choke

63

myself: there's all I'll do for you" (I.v.86-87), is his response to her offer. Within the frame story, love will defeat hate; the fairy tale will have the ending wished for by Imogen's sympathizers at court. One of them prays for Imogen:

> Betwixt a father by thy step-dame govern'd,
> A mother hourly coining plots, a wooer
> More hateful than the foul expulsion is
> Of thy dear husband, than that horrid act
> Of the divorce he'ld make!   The heavens hold firm
> The walls of thy dear honour, keep unshaked
> That temple, thy fair mind, that thou mayst stand,
> To enjoy thy banish'd lord and this great land!   (II.i.63-70)

Imogen's domestic enemies have hard hearts, but, Shakespeare shows, their weapons are blunt. He suggests the peculiar effectiveness of calumny by setting the wager plot within a story in which more primitive persecutors fail.[7] By the time Posthumus and Iachimo have settled on their stakes in Rome, it is clear that the real menace is not in the queen's drugs, but in the Italian villain's subtler poison.

The gambling incident in *Cymbeline*—in contrast with Boccaccio's—owes much to the ethical tradition which we have examined. In the *Decameron* the merchants' conversation leads from one "trifle" to the next, and on the subject of their wives' unchastity their aim is to outjest one another. Bernardo, the only one who takes ideas of honor and chastity seriously, is the butt of Ambrogiuolo's sarcastic witticisms. Against his idealism the prevailing assumption is that all women are the same, flesh and blood; infidelity, being natural, is not disgraceful. To comic effect Boccaccio alludes to a convention from the slandered woman tradition, as Bernardo offers his life against the villain's gold florins that his wife will prove true. The realist rejoins, "if I had won the wager, I know not what I should doe with thy head." Even though the other merchants try "to breake the wager, knowing great harm must needs ensue thereon," the scene is almost wholly comic.[8] The subject of honor is trivial to everyone except the target of the hilarity. In *Frederyke* the scene is less cynical in tone, but here too the merchants' consensus is that their wives in their absence "eate and drynke of the beste . . . and so get they unto them hote bloud and than they may take another lystye yong man and do their pleasure with him. . . ."[9] Only Ambrosius, the hero, is disturbed by the tenor of the conversation.

Not only does Shakespeare relinquish the comic effects achieved by Boccaccio, but he magnifies the element of potential tragedy in the situation. Ideas of honor, reputation, good and ill opinion and evil-speaking become momen-

64

tous as Posthumus and Iachimo debate. What are merely undertones in the original wager scene become crucial themes in *Cymbeline,* and the jests of the Boccaccian merchants are echoed only to intensify Shakespeare's "graver purpose." The dramatist prepares carefully for the wager episode. Before Posthumus comes onstage to meet the antagonist, three characters are discussing him; for the second time we listen to a conversation about his reputation. In the opening scene of the play, one gentleman had praised Posthumus to another, "[speaking] him far" and referring to Imogen's opinion of him:

> to his mistress,
> For whom he now is banish'd, her own price
> Proclaims how she esteem'd him and his virtue;
> By her election may be truly read
> What kind of man he is.   (I.i.50-54)

The second gentleman had recognized the significance of Imogen's estimation, had added his own praise solely on the strength of others':

> I honour him
> Even out of your report.   (I.i.54-55)

The interchange suggests the traditional meaning of fame, the sense that honor is a true reflection of virtue.

Now in Rome a more skeptical discussion of the subject is underway. The world may honor Posthumus, but Iachimo reserves his praise: "Believe it, sir, I have seen him in Britain: he was then of a crescent note, expected to prove so worthy as since he hath been allowed the name of; but I could then have looked on him without the help of admiration, though the catalogue of his endowments had been tabled by his side and I to peruse him by items" (I.iv.1-7). And the honor which has come to Posthumus because of Imogen is probably undeserved, the villain continues: "This matter of marrying his king's daughter, wherein he must be weighed rather by her value than his own, words him, I doubt not, a great deal from the matter" (I.iv.14-17). And finally—his reasoning circular—Iachimo condemns the princess for her opinion: " . . . the approbation of those that weep this lamentable divorce under her colours are wonderfully to extend him; be it but to fortify her judgement, which else an easy battery might lay flat, for taking a beggar without less quality" (I.iv.19-23). These comments reveal the villain's valuation of good name. Since the beginning of the play, Shakespeare has introduced opposing views of honor, setting Iachimo's sense of its insignificance against the two gentlemen's traditional view. Now as Posthumus enters and the talk turns toward the subject of Imogen's chastity, the collision between Posthumus' "confidence" in his wife and the "ill opinion" of the skeptic demonstrates that the importance of the issue is literally mortal.

Shakespeare's wager scene begins as the Frenchman recollects that Posthumus had once nearly risked his life affirming "his to be more fair, virtuous, wise, chaste, constant-qualified and less attemptable than any the rarest of our ladies in France" (I.iv.62-66). The speaker had reconciled Posthumus and his opponent, and now reflects that "it had been pity you should have been put together with so mortal a purpose as then each bore, upon importance of so slight and trivial a nature" (I.iv.42-45). Imogen's husband still believes, " . . . my quarrel was not altogether slight" (I.iv.51). He had asserted her truth "upon warrant of bloody affirmation" (I.iv.62) and would do so again. Now Shakespeare's villain offers his challenge, "That lady is not now living or this gentleman's opinion by this worn out" (I.iv.67-68), and the notion that the topic is trivial begins to recede. Iachimo is not joking, as Posthumus guesses. This interchange directs attention to the idea that the spoken word, unless it is completely meaningless, has a life and power of its own:

> *Post.* This is but a custom in your tongue; you bear a graver purpose, I hope.
> *Iach.* I am the master of my speeches, and would undergo what's spoken, I swear.
> *Post.* Will you? I shall but lend my diamond till your return: let there be covenants drawn between 's: my mistress exceeds in goodness the hugeness of your unworthy thinking: I dare you to this match: here's my ring.

(I.iv.150-58)

The husband sets forth the great opposites, truth and ill opinion. Money and jewelry already hazarded, Posthumus enters blood into the contract: "I embrace these conditions; let us have articles betwixt us. Only, thus far you shall answer: if you make your voyage upon her and give me directly to understand you have prevailed, I am no further your enemy; she is not worth our debate: if she remain unseduced, you not making it appear otherwise, for your ill opinion and the assault you have made to her chastity you shall answer me with your sword" (I.iv.168-76). The dominant idea in this wager scene is completely non-Boccaccian. That Imogen has been wronged by the villain's ill opinion and by his words, that her defamation is an act of destruction and not merely inconsequential talk, is a sense quite incongruous with the source material. The gambling scene in the French play, although much simpler, is similarly solemn. Lands are wagered after the hero has reproached the villain for speaking ill of women: "Par foy, Berengier, c'est mau dit / Dire des dames villenie" (658-59).

66

Both plays deviate from the typical wager pattern by presenting a scene in which the villain assails the heroine's honor. In contrast, the prose analogues bear out Greenlaw's observation that wager stories tend to obscure the seduction attempt (characteristic of the elemental slandered woman story) "in order to gain interest for the stratagem by which the proofs are to be obtained."[10] Boccaccio's villain, investigating Genevra's reputation in Genoa, finds that Bernardo's wife is "reputed to be the onely wonder of women; whereby he plainely perceived that he had undertaken a very idle enterprise."[11] He sets to work on the trick which will enable him to appear the winner of the bet. He does not even see Genevra until the night he climbs out of the chest in her bedroom while she sleeps; then he dares not approach her. In *Frederyke*, the villain speaks to the woman but makes no effort to win her. Impressed by her modest manner, he sees that he has lost the bet. "For she semeth a worshypfull woman and I dare not speke to her of that vylany, whereof I am sory."[12] These wagerers, furtive and timid, think only momentarily of confronting the heroines.

But the miracle play and *Cymbeline* re-enact the judges' assault on Susanna. Berengier tells Denise that her husband has betrayed her, and professing deep concern for her and anger at her beloved's behavior, he offers her his love: "L'amour de vous m'a si espris / Que nuit ne jour ne puis durer, / Tant me fait griefs maulx endurer / Pour vous, ma dame" (726-41). Denise indignantly rebukes him for his wickedness and treason, disbelieving him immediately. She dismisses him angrily:

> Conment, Berengier?   Par vostre ame,
> Estes vous un si vaillant homme
> Que venez jusques cy de Romme
> Pour moy dire ai fait langage?
> Certes vous ne vostre lignage
> Ne sariez dire un seul bien, non,
> Fors mauvaistié et traison;
> Et pour ce de rien ne vous croy.
> Vuidiez, vuidiez, de devant moy
>   Isnel le pas.   (742-51)

And Iachimo does his best to seduce Imogen. The scene, Furness noticed, is quite like the one in the miracle.[13] Not only does it set the accuser and his victim against each other dramatically, but it also underlines the theme of false report. And Shakespeare deepens the seriousness of the conversation by keeping in our minds another ethical perspective, alluding to the kind of cynical amusement with which Boccaccio's merchants had regarded the subject of adultery. Iachimo describes the banished husband who, he claims, has earned the name of "Briton reveller" in Rome. We may be hearing echoes of laughter from the *Decameron* in this elaborate prevarication:

> I never saw him sad.
> There is a Frenchman his companion, one
> An eminent monsieur, that, it seems, much loves
> A Gallian girl at home; he furnaces
> The thick sighs from him whiles the jolly Briton—
> Your lord, I mean—laughs from's free lungs, cries 'O,
> Can my sides hold, to think that man, who knows
> By history, report, or his own proof,
> What woman is, yea, what she cannot choose
> But must be, will his free hours languish for
> Assured bondage?' (I.vi.63-73)

This account of the conversation which led to the wager between idealistic lover and cynic, we know, is not only untrue; it is a perfect inversion of the truth. This slanderer uses Iago's techniques, feigning reluctance to bring bad news so that Imogen must ask, "discover to me / What both you spur and stop" (I.vi.98-99). He is a consummate liar; his report is vivid, his feigned outrage convincing. "Had I this cheek / To bathe my lips upon," he muses,

> should I, damn'd then,
> Slaver with lips as common as the stairs
> That mount the Capitol; join gripes with hands
> Made hard with hourly falsehood—falsehood, as
> With labour; then by-peeping in an eye
> Base and unlustrous as the smoky light
> That's fed with stinking tallow; it were fit
> That all the plagues of hell should at one time
> Encounter such revolt. (I.vi.99-112)

Imogen is quiet; "My lord, I fear, / Has forgot Britain," she says, and then, as had her French counterpart, "Let me hear no more" (I.vi.112-17). But Iachimo suggests that she take revenge ("I dedicate myself to your sweet pleasure" [I.vi.136]), and Imogen soon understands his purpose. She sends him away with a clear verdict on the bearer of false witness.

> Away! I do condemn mine ears that have
> So long attended thee.   If thou were honourable,
> Thou wouldst have told this tale for virtue, not
> For such an end thou seek'st—as base as strange.
> Thou wrong'st a gentleman who is as far
> From thy report as thou from honour, and
> Solicit'st here a lady that disdains
> Thee, and the devil alike. (I.vi.141-48)

For the moment the slanderer has met his match, in Imogen's faith; the accusation backfires. Her condemnation echoes Posthumus' earlier anger at the villain's "unworthy thinking." Her sense that the spoken falsehood is itself a great wrong, whether credited or not, is in keeping with the tradition familiar to us.

Cymbeline and the French play set forth in these scenes the vast opposition between slander and love. Iachimo's inversions of truth especially accentuate the moral contrarieties in the story, insist that we "Partition make," in Iachimo's own words, "... 'Twixt fair and foul" (I.vi.38). Significantly, Shakespeare's villain thinks (as had his counterparts in the prose stories) when he sees the woman whom he will later malign,

> All of her that is out of door most rich!
> If she be furnish'd with a mind so rare,
> She is alone the Arabian bird, and I
> Have lost the wager. (I.vi.15-18)

This perception intensifies his later shame at having "belied a lady" (V.ii.2). The repentant Iachimo tells Cymbeline,

> ... I was taught
> Of your chaste daughter the wide difference
> 'Twixt amorous and villainous. (V.v.193-95)

This wide difference is what the confrontations between the heroines and their defamers in these plays are designed to display. In creating the attempted seduction, Shakespeare points up themes typically blurred in wager stories.[14]

His characterization of Pisanio serves the same purpose. The story as he found it in the *Decameron* and *Frederyke* contains a servant who is commanded by the husband to kill the supposed adulteress but fails to do so. Shakespeare made the servant's role much more positive. Pisanio is like Beatrice, Emilia, and Paulina; and he has a counterpart in the French wager play, an anonymous citizen. These figures are purveyors of True Report; they believe in the heroines and work to preserve their lives. They stand in conscious moral opposition to the slander—while the servants in the sources of *Cymbeline* are unaware of it.

Boccaccio's Bernardo commands a trusted servant to conduct Genevra out of Genoa, instructing him, "whenas he should be with the lady in such a place as should seem best to him, to put her to death without pity and return to him." Bringing the woman past a desolate place, the servant tells her that she must die. She asks "wherein I have offended thee, and why thou must kill me?"; he explains, "Alas good Mistresse ... you have not any way offended

69

me, but in what occasion you have displeased your Husband, it is utterly unknowne to me: for he hath strictly commanded me, without respect of pitty or compassion, to kill you by the way as I bring you, and if I doe it not, he hath sworne to hang me by the necke. You know good Mistresse, how much I stand obliged to him, and how impossible it is for me, to contradict any thing that he commandeth. God is my witnesse, that I am truly compassionate of you, and yet (by no meanes) may I let you live." The story-teller engages our interest in the servant's position and viewpoint, in his conflicting feelings of fear, obligation, pity. Dramatic irony stems from both characters' ignorance. Genevra asks for mercy, avowing, "God . . . is my faithfull witnesse, that I never committed any offence, whereby to deserve the dislike of my Husband, much lesse so harsh a recompense as this is." But quickly she thinks of a way in which the servant, while sparing her, can bring evidence of her death to Bernardo. The servant, "who had no great good will to kill her, very easily grew pittifull."[15] Because of Genevra's cleverness, she and the servant both escape punishment. In *Frederyke* the incident unfolds in much the same way. The servant knows nothing about the slander but decides upon receiving the order from his master that "it was better to slee his maystress than his selfe to be slayne." "My maister hath charged me," he tells the bewildered heroine, "upon payne of death that I should slee you here and bryng to hym for a token your tongue and a locke of youre heere."[16] The woman suggests the substitution of her pet lamb's tongue and the scheme works just as it does in the *Decameron*. Both servants are relieved when the heroines help them but had, however reluctantly, intended to carry out their orders.

But in *Cymbeline* and its distant dramatic analogue these figures have definite thematic significance. In the miracle the Troisiesme Bourgois, hearing about the wager, takes it upon himself to befriend Denise. He rides for six straight days to warn her that her husband intends to kill her. When she asks, "pour quoy?" qu'ay je meffait? / Scez tu, amis?" (986-87), he tells her the story of the wager and the villain's boast that he had won it:

> Et oultre tout ce fist il dyables,
> Qu'enseignes apporta creables,
> > Dont me merveil. (1005-07)

When she answers that she has been defamed, the man offers compassion and advice:

> Chiére dame, prenez confort
> En vous mesmes, et regardez
> Conment vostre vie gardez:
> > Je le conseil. (1014-17)

The citizen's part is small, but crucial. Because of his spontaneous faith the slandered heroine learns of her situation. Because of his warning she prays to the Virgin for guidance and Nostre Dame comes to comfort and aid her. Pisanio's faith is likewise instrumental in preserving Imogen's life.

In Act III Pisanio enters with Posthumus' letter instructing him to kill Imogen as a "strumpet."[17] Shakespeare achieves an irony more complicated than that which in the sources arises from the servants' ignorance. For he gives Pisanio an intuitive "knowledge" of the truth which is, in fact, not knowledge, but the faith of love. Without hesitation he condemns the letter's sender, recognizing the accusation for exactly what it is:

> How? of adultery?   Wherefore write you not
> What monster's her accuser?   Leonatus!
> O master!   what a strange infection
> Is fall'n into thy ear!   What false Italian,
> As poisonous-tongued as handed, hath prevail'd
> On thy too ready hearing?   Disloyal!   No:
> She's punish'd for her truth, and undergoes,
> More goddess-like than wife-like, such assaults
> As would take in some virtue.   O my master!
> Thy mind to her is now as low as were
> Thy fortunes.   How! That I should murder her?
> Upon the love and truth and vows which I
> Have made to thy command?   I, her?   Her blood?
> If it be so to do good service, never
> Let me be counted serviceable.   How look I,
> That I should seem to lack humanity
> So much as this fact comes to?   (III.ii.1-17)

Pisanio's surmises are, we know, the precise truth. He voices the traditional sense that slander monstrously, treacherously strikes at virtue, and that to give ear to false report is deep sin. While his counterparts in the *Decameron* and *Frederyke* are perplexed by contradictory moral feelings, Pisanio's mind is clear. He refuses to consider following the order just as he had earlier defied the evil queen. The speech explicitly lines up the great moral oppositions in the play, between the poisoned tongue and our very humanity.

This servant, like the citizen in the miracle play, takes upon himself the painful burden of telling the heroine about her situation. He hands Imogen the letter:

> Please you read,
> And you shall find me, wretched man, a thing
> The most disdain'd of fortune.   (III.iv.18-20)

Watching her read it, he thinks, "What shall I need to draw my sword? /

The paper hath cut her throat already." Then in lines which glance back over centuries, he speaks of the calumny:

> ... 'tis slander,
> Whose edge is sharper than the sword, whose tongue
> Outvenoms all the worms of Nile, whose breath
> Rides on the posting winds and doth belie
> All corners of the world: kings, queens, and states,
> Maids, matrons, nay, the secrets of the grave
> This viperous slander enters.   (III.iv.34-41)

Nowhere in Shakespeare is there a more evocative expression of slander's profound ruinousness. The diction is predominantly his own; while the sharp sword is borrowed from the tradition, the Egyptian worm and the "posting winds" are new. And here is a "modern" version of Gower's list ("Et piere et miere et soer germeine, / Moigne, Frere, Canoun, Noneine," etc.) of those whom this quick assassin destroys. The speaker saves Imogen's life, despite her demand that he follow the letter's instructions. She wants to die, saying that there can be no life, no "comfort, when I am / Dead to my husband" (III.iv.132-33). She condemns Posthumus' treachery, his failure of faith. She asks Pisanio to hit her heart:

> Fear not; 'tis empty of all things but grief:
> Thy master is not there, who was indeed
> The riches of it.   (III.iv.71-73)

This looks forward to Hermione's statement that life is valueless when love and faith are lost. Here, it is only because of Pisanio that Imogen has the heart to go on; she follows his plan for her survival. He is like True Report and the citizen who rides from far away to help Denise. This sequence in *Cymbeline* is utterly different from the incidents in which the Boccaccian heroines plead and bargain for their lives with vacillating servants.

In Shakespeare's wager story and the miracle play, divine intervention brings the truth to light and makes possible the happy ending; resolution in the prose analogues is brought about by human effort, by the resourcefulness of the heroines. From the moment Genevra escapes death by creating the disguise scheme, Boccaccio emphasizes her cleverness. She capitalizes on her man's role, achieves high status in service to the Sultan, and takes advantage of the accidents by which she learns about the wager. After finally understanding "the occasion of her husband's hatred to her,"[18] Genevra sets the villain up in business in order to follow his movements until she can send for Bernardo. Then she traps him into confessing everything. The scene is climaxed by her revelation that she is Genevra; the villain is sentenced to death; the heroine receives all Ambrogiuolo's worldly possessions and much more gold, silver and money. Through ingenuity and perseverance, she has outwitted her detractor. The woman in *Frederyke* is similarly adroit in managing her own deliverance. Imogen and Denise suffer with strength and dignity, but their helplessness is emphasized. They are exhausted and heartsick.

The participation of divine characters, a feature consistent with the defenselessness of the slandered women, is the most remarkable parallel between Shakespeare's play and the French one. It was noticed long ago,[19] but its importance has not perhaps been appreciated. The appearance of Jupiter—on the face of it a somewhat odd feature of *Cymbeline*—serves to stress the preternatural power of slander, as does the Virgin Mary's role in the miracle. The French hero progresses from unfounded wrath to repentance solely through divine agency. Unable to find his wife because the Troisiesme Bourgois and the Virgin Mary have placed her beyond his reach, he renounces God:

> Je croy que Dieux a elle part:
> Ce fait mon, je le voy tresbien.
> Ha! mauvais Dieu, que ne te tien!
> Vraiement, se je te tenoie,
> De cops tout te desromperoie.
> Egar! voiz: toy et ta creance
> Reni et toute ta puissance,
> Et si m'en vois droit oultre mer
> Conme Sarrazin demourer
> Et tenir la loy Mahommet;
> Car qui en toy s'entente met
>   Il fait folie   (1299-1310)

That the deceived hero deserts God because the heroine is receiving divine aid powerfully reinforces the evil of his delusion. But toward the end of the play he spontaneously regrets his apostacy:

> Elas! chetis! que fas je cy?
> Je pers mon temps et mon corps; voire,
> Je pers m'ame, je pers la gloire
> Des cieulx que je deusse acquerre.
> Las! se le cuer de dueil me serre,
> J'ay raison et cause trop bonne.
> Bien sui malostrue personne,
> Qui en tel servage me met
> Qui je sers et croy Mahommet,
> Qui n'est que droite fanfelue.   (1501-10)

He asks for mercy and forgiveness. In a vision God tells him that he has wronged Denise, that he must ask for her pardon: "... tu as un grant deffault, / Qu'a tort as ta femme hay / Et jusques a mort envay" (1573-80). Restored to his proper relationship with God, the hero subsequently vanquishes the villain in combat and forces him to confess. The play has defined belief in the false accusation as deep sin indeed, and only a celestial vision has enabled the sinner to become undeceived, to regain faith. In the prose versions the hero recognizes the truth only after the facts have been laid bare, the villain's device exposed.

Posthumus' progress from anger to repentance is strikingly similar. It is unprepared for, "unrealistic," illogical. It is not paralleled in Boccaccio, although in *Frederyke*, after the servant brings evidence of the heroine's death, the husband is "more sorier than he was before, because that he spake not with her before that he caused her to be put to death, to examyne her wherfore John of Florence had the Jewels."[20] Posthumus too is suddenly filled with anguish because he has caused Imogen's death, even though he still thinks her guilty. He believes that he is more blameworthy than she:

> Gods! if you
> Should have ta'en vengeance on my faults, I never
> Had lived to put on this: so had you saved
> The noble Imogen to repent, and struck
> Me, wretch more worth your vengeance. (V.i.7-11)

The facts known to us are yet to be revealed to Posthumus, and so this total reversal in his attitude—seemingly unmotivated—has dissatisfied many critics of *Cymbeline*. It seems to Nosworthy "contrary to the moral code of the play." But the hero's grief and especially his self-castigation develop a suggestion in *Much Ado* that comes from the priest, who predicts that after Hero's death Claudio will "wish he had not so accused her, / No, though he thought his accusation true" (IV.i.234-35). Posthumus' speech and the sequence in the miracle play focus on the intrinsic wickedness of the accusation. Even though one may object, with Nosworthy, that since Posthumus "still believes in Imogen's guilt, his attitude toward her should remain unchanged, however much he may repent of the supposed murder,"[21] Shakespeare, I believe, wants to emphasize the absolute seriousness of Posthumus' "great fail." Iachimo's repentance fits the play in the same way, after an incident reminiscent of the combat which frequently concludes slander plots.

Posthumus, although brought to England with Roman troops, fights on behalf of his dead wife:

> ... I'll die
> For thee, O Imogen, even for whom my life
> Is every breath a death; and thus, unknown,
> Pitied nor hated, to the face of peril
> Myself I'll dedicate.   (V.i.25-29)

The unknown champion thinks of his role in the war as symbolic; and Iachimo takes his defeat at the hands of Posthumus, whom he does not recognize, as retribution for his crime against Imogen:

> The heaviness and guilt within my bosom
> Takes off my manhood: I have belied a lady,
> The princess of this country, and the air on 't
> Revengingly enfeebles me; or could this carl,
> A very drudge of nature's, have subdued me
> In my profession?   (V.ii.1-6)

Shakespeare could have untwisted the plot with a forced confession like Boccaccio's; Imogen recognizes her ring on Iachimo after the battle is over and the facts emerge then. But instead—pointing to his theme—he gives the villain a sense that the combat is a moral verdict.

Shakespeare's *deus ex machina*, analogous to the miracles in *Susanna* and the French play, is far different from the plotting which in the sources makes discovery inevitable.[22] Jupiter's intervention near the end of the drama suggests that the playwright is concerned less with psychological consistency at this point than with the theme of lost and regained faith. Jupiter predicts the ending, that Posthumus "shall be lord of lady Imogen, / And happier much by his affliction made" (V.iv.107-08). As we have seen, the idea that only a miracle can winnow the truth from slander is traditional. The historical definition of detraction and the conventions of the accused woman tale provide a more precise explanation than has yet been offered for Jupiter's presence in *Cymbeline*.[23]

Marvels, symbolic combats, and prophetic visions from heaven do not fit the worldly realm of the wager story as it was rendered in the sources of *Cymbeline*. But Jupiter's thunderous descent, like Shakespeare's other innovations (the new setting, the seduction scene, the heroic servant), directs our attention to the ethical essentials in the story. I believe that the resemblances beween *Cymbeline* and the remote French analogue are most important. In both dramas "modern" material is given an old arrangement: hence, the incongruities in Shakespeare's treatment.[24] His villain, especially, is caught between two worlds; the Iachimo of the wager scene is too realistic to fit

75

perfectly the part of the penitent in Act Five. Shakespeare used Boccaccio's starting mechanism because motive was not to matter especially in *Cymbeline*; he departed from his predecessors in bringing to the center of his wager play the themes of ill thinking and false speech.[25] In *The Winter's Tale* he went even further in this direction, creating a kind of vacuum where motive had been in order to focus on consequence entirely.

CHAPTER FIVE

"The Injury of Tongues": Slander in *The Winter's Tale*

In *The Winter's Tale* Shakespeare expresses with ultimate clarity the perfect antithesis between slander and love. Here there is no villainy like Iago's or Iachimo's; instead slander, the effect of unfounded jealousy, seems to come from nowhere. So we focus on the ruinous power of the false utterance itself and watch while another paradise is destroyed, even though there is no serpent. We grieve for the hero-slanderer as much as for his victim; but unlike Othello he gets another chance, gains "clearer knowledge" (II.i.97) before it is entirely too late. With "the injury of tongues" (I.ii.338) its central theme, *The Winter's Tale* is as radical a transformation of its source as any of Shakespeare's other slander plays.

In *Pandosto* Greene takes up a wide variety of themes. Through soliloquies and conversations he examines such issues as a servant's duty to his master versus his conscience, the propriety of love between a prince and a shepherdess, the relative values of honesty and wealth. In his antithetical style he balances contradictory ideas and feelings; thematic interests diffuse. The heroine's monologue on defamation is an instructive example. Bellaria, after learning from a public proclamation that her husband has accused her of adultery, first complains that noble birth and high place have made her vulnerable to Fortune. Then the slandered woman begins to contemplate the meaning of the situation: "Thou art . . . accused without cause, and therefore oughtest to dye without care: for patience is a shield against Fortune, and a guiltless minde yeeldeth not to sorrow." She is momentarily consoled by this thought, only to be disturbed by another: "Ah, but Infamie galleth unto death, and liveth after death: Report is plumed with Times feathers, and Envie oftentimes soundeth Fames trumpet: the suspected adulterie shall fly in the ayre, and thy knowne vertues shall ly hid in the Earth; one Moale staineth a whole face; and what is once spotted with Infamy can hardly be worne out with time." This traditional conception, that the effects of slander are positive and irremediable, puts Bellaria in a desperate mood. But then her stoicism returns as she considers the extrinsic quality of honor: "Pandosto hath darkened thy fame, but shal never discredite thy vertues. Suspition may enter a false action, but proofs shall never put in his plea: care not then for envie, sith report hath a blister on her tongue: and let sorrow baite them which offend, not touch thee that art faultlesse."[1] Thus she is drawn alternately to each side of the debate, and the issue is left hanging in the balance. In this way Greene surveys at least two sides of any given subject. His characters' thoughts are usually "sundry," just as thematic concerns in the romance as a whole are various.

Shakespeare's artistic scheme is completely different. Out of Greene's narrative the playwright takes what enhances the theme of the slandered woman, concentrates on it, and discards the rest. In writing the story of Hermione and Leontes he reduces Greene's assortment of motifs to one urgent theme, and by eliminating debate on this theme, he achieves even greater compression. The meaning of Hermione's case is not at issue, but has become a given. In *The Winter's Tale* "Infamie galleth unto death"; there is no alleviation. Honor in its traditional sense, the "testemonie of vertue shining of yt self, geven of some man by the iudgment of good men,"[2] is valued absolutely. It is at the heart of social life, more precious than life itself. In attacking Hermione's name, Leontes is striking at what ties her to the community. And so his sin is deadly indeed. Shakespeare's departures from his source serve to enhance all this, and to express more economically than ever before the antithesis between detraction and love.

Leontes' lack of motivation has been much discussed. Having explored in *Othello* the question of how groundless jealousy could grow in a noble heart, Shakespeare merely postulates Leontes' irrational suspicion. Pandosto's "certaine melancholy passion" enters his mind with some reason and takes hold of it by degrees. Bellaria, "willing to show how unfaynedly shee looved her husband by his friends intertainment, used him likewise so familiarly, that her countenance bewraied how her minde was affected towardes him: oftentimes comming her selfe into his bed chamber, to see that nothing should be amis to mislike him." Greene emphasizes Bellaria's hospitality, the "honest familiarity" between wife and friend which "increased dayly more and more" until "there grew such a secret uniting of their affections, that the one could not well be without the company of the other." When Pandosto's state affairs occupy him, Bellaria and Egistus walk in the garden, "where they two in privat and pleasant devises would passe away the time to both their contents" (p. 158). Pandosto's misinterpretation of appearances is understandable. After being driven into "sundry and doubtfull thoughts," the king deliberates carefully. Considerations about his wife's beauty and his friend's comeliness, speculations about the nature of fancy, friendship and love, "a long time smoothering in his stomacke, beganne at last to kindle in his minde a secret mistrust, which increased by suspition, grewe at last to be a flaming Jealousie, that so tormented him as he could take no rest." Even now he attempts to gain certainty by watching the pair more carefully, but of course the two "seely soules" continue to frequent each other's company daily until he is driven into a "franticke passion." Finally sure that he has been betrayed, Pandosto "devis[es] with himself a long time" and determines to have his friend poisoned (p. 159). The account of the inception and growth of Pandosto's jealousy is a sympathetic one. His observations and deductions, though mistaken, seem valid to the reader.

Shakespeare's treatment of Leontes' jealousy boldly defies psychological probability. The dramatist emphasizes the strength of the bond between Leontes and Polixenes; we think, with Polixenes' servant, "there is not in the world either malice or matter to alter it" (I.i.36-37). And indeed there is not. Leontes' idea that Hermione has deceived him is a "dream," Shakespeare emphasizes, based on "faith" rather than fact of any kind, even an appearance or report. There is no tale of a window-scene, no handkerchief trick, no description of a bedroom or birthmark. This terrible error is pure illusion, and a self-engendered, spontaneous illusion at that; there has been no villain to perform the sleight of hand. And Leontes is not malicious; he feels no envy, no joy in others' grief; nor does he intentionally lie. He defames his wife because his opinion is "diseased."

Realistic psychological foundation and traditional spiritual explanation stripped away, what remains in *The Winter's Tale* is slander itself. Leontes' thoughts and words are merely untrue. Hermione says, upon hearing his accusation:

> Should a villain say so,
> The most replenish'd villain in the world,
> He were as much more villain: you, my lord,
> Do but mistake.   (II.i.78-81)

In this last of his plays about slander Shakespeare has made cause immaterial in order to dwell on effect, has made us look at the grown delusion rather than "question how 'tis born" (I.ii.433). In doing so he dramatizes the sense that had been at the core of the allegorical tradition: that irrespective of its origin, slander resembles envy in its effect. Mistaken rather than malicious, Leontes nevertheless speaks in envy's tongue. "I am galled," he says; and the thought of his "sullied sheets" is "goads, thorns, nettles, tails of wasps . . ." (I.ii.316; 328-29). The destruction in *The Winter's Tale* is the same as that for which the traditional villains are responsible. Love and lives are lost, and the slanderer himself suffers dreadfully. Says Camillo, toward the end:

79

My lord, your sorrow was too sore laid on,
Which sixteen winters cannot blow away,
So many summers dry: scarce any joy
Did ever so long live; no sorrow
But kill'd itself much sooner.   (V.ii.49-53)

All this ensues from "folly," senseless but stubborn. By giving Leontes' jealousy a pathological quality the playwright keeps us from asking "How should this grow?" (I.ii.431) and compels our undistracted attention to "the werste vice of alle."

Shakespeare modifies the role of the servant in *Pandosto* much as he had altered the Boccaccian servant for *Cymbeline*. Again the source presents a character commanded to kill, but ignorant of the reason for the order. After deciding that Egistus must die, Pandosto "called upon him his cupbearer, with whom in secret he brake the matter: promising to him for the performance thereof to geve him a thousande crownes of yearely revenues." Franion attempts to dissuade the king, but Greene stops short of explaining why, giving the reader two quite different choices: the servant is "eyther ... of a good conscience, or willing for fashion sake, to deny such a bloudy request. ... " Franion's arguments are about the offensiveness of murder and "causeless cruelty," about the obligations of friendship and respect for kings. He points out that if Pandosto should now murder his friend without reason, "it would not only be a great dishonor to his Majesty, and a meanes to sow perpetuall enmitie betweene the Sycilians and the Bohemians, but also his owne subjectes would repine at such trecherous crueltie." But, "seeing that to perswade Pandosto any more, was but to strive against the streame," Franion pretends to consent to the plan. Secretly he thinks about whether he should carry out the instructions which are essentially meaningless to him. In a long internal debate he balances opposing moral claims: "Thou art servant to a king, and must obey at commaund: yet Franion, against law and conscience, it is not good to resist a tyrant with armes, nor to please an unjust king with obedience. What shalt thou do? Folly refused gold, and frensie preferment: wisedome seeketh after dignitie, and counsel looketh for gaine" (p. 160). Not knowing why Pandosto suddenly wants his friend dead, the servant can consider the ethics of the situation only theoretically. At one point he is about to conclude, "Care not then though most count thee a traytor, so all call thee rich. Dignitie (Franion) advanceth thy posteritie, and evile report can hurt but thyselfe" (p. 161). Yet finally conscience wins out, and he chooses a clear mind before dignity; poverty and peace over wealth and disquiet. When he warns Egistus of his danger and promises to flee with him, Egistus concludes that Pandosto is planning to make war on him. The thematic interests scatter further, as Egistus, "hearing the solemne protestation of Franion, began to consider, that in love and kingdomes, neither faith, nor lawe is to bee respected: doubting that Pandosto thought by his death to destroy his men, and with speedy warre to invade Sycilia. These and such doubtes throughly weighed, he gave great thankes to Franion . . . " (p. 162). Greene's unknowing servant and mystified king provide Greene with opportunities for reflection on many subjects; Bellaria's plight is left suspended, for the moment, in the background. Shakespeare keeps Hermione's upstage; he gives Camillo knowledge of Leontes' delusion and makes him a central character, a bearer of true report.

In a speech full of coarse language Leontes commands his servant to agree that Hermione "deserves a name / As rank as any flax-wench that puts to / Before her trothplight." Instead Camillo condemns Leontes' words, voicing the traditional theme:

> I would not be a stander-by to hear
> My sovereign mistress clouded so, without
> My present vengeance taken: 'shrew my heart,
> You never spoke what did become you less
> Than this; which to reiterate were sin
> As deep as that, though true.   (I.ii.267-84)

The irony in the speaker's assumption that someone has misled Leontes emphasizes the king's twisted perception. The power of detraction against goodness is clearly exemplified in this play within the hero himself, for, as Camillo sees, his base opinion constitutes a "rebellion" (I.ii.355) against his own nobility. The loyal servant tries helplessly to mend the error, begging Leontes, "Good my lord, be cured / Of this diseased opinion, and betimes; / For 'tis most dangerous." But truth, we know, is no defense against calumny:

> *Leon.*   Say it be, 'tis true.
> *Cam.*   No, no, my lord.
> *Leon.*   It is; you lie, you lie:
> I say thou liest, Camillo, and I hate thee,
> Pronounce thee a gross lout, a mindless slave,
> Or else a hovering temporizer, that
> Canst with thine eyes at once see good and evil,
> Inclining to them both.   (I.ii.296-304)

The description fits Greene's servant but not Shakespeare's. Shakespeare gives Camillo instinctive faith and moral clearsightedness, and the good and evil he sees are the ethical opposites at the heart of the story. Explaining why he cannot participate in Leontes' plan, Camillo repeats:

81

> ... I cannot
> Believe this crack to be in my dread mistress,
> So sovereignly being honourable.
> I have loved thee,—

At the mention of slander's traditional antidote, Leontes angers: "Make that thy question, and go rot!" (I.ii.321-24).

Camillo's soliloquy and his conversation with Polixenes reflect the theme of defamation. Franion's internal vacillation about whether or not to kill Egistus becomes in *The Winter's Tale* a strong comment on the ethical meaning of Leontes' fantasy:

> O miserable lady! But, for me,
> What case stand I in? I must be the poisoner
> Of good Polixenes; and my ground to do't
> Is the obedience to a master, one
> Who in rebellion with himself will have
> All that are his so too. To do this deed,
> Promotion follows. If I could find example
> Of thousands that had struck anointed kings
> And flourish'd after, I'ld not do't; but since
> Nor brass nor stone nor parchment bears not one,
> Let villany itself forswear't. (I.ii.351-61)

The characterization of Camillo keeps the moral lines of the story clear. His conversation with Polixenes is devoid of the suspicions and psychological complexities that interest Greene. When he reveals Leontes' suspicion to Polixenes, he emphasizes its irrationality:

> Swear his thought over
> By each particular star in heaven and
> By all their influences, you may as well
> Forbid the sea for to obey the moon
> As or by oath remove or counsel shake
> The fabric of his folly, whose foundation
> Is piled upon his faith and will continue
> The standing of his body. (I.ii.424-31)

Whereas Polixenes' counterpart in Greene first suspects the servant of treachery and then concludes that his friend's sudden enmity is political, Polixenes says simply, "I do believe thee: / I saw his heart in 's face. Give me thy hand" (I.ii.446-47). Polixenes' further reflections on the astonishing news are tinged with fear, underlining the momentousness of dishonor:

> This jealousy
> Is for a precious creature: as she's rare,
> Must it be great, and as his person's mighty,

Must it be violent, and as he does conceive
He is dishonour'd by a man which ever
Profess'd to him, why, his revenges must
In that be made more bitter.   Fear o'ershades me:
Good expedition be my friend, and comfort
The gracious queen, part of his theme, but nothing
Of his ill-ta'en suspicion!   (I.ii.451-60)

Shakespeare uses Camillo's conversations with the hero and his friend to point to theme; what is obscure to Greene's characters is perfectly understood by Shakespeare's. Truth in all its transparent simplicity surrounds the mistaken hero.

The accusation scene in *The Winter's Tale* is the dramatist's invention, inspired by two separate passages in Greene's narrative. Pandosto, convinced that his cupbearer, his wife, and his friend have all conspired against him, commands that the queen be imprisoned. "The guarde, unwilling to lay their hands on such a vertuous Princesse, and yet fearing the kings furie, went very sorrowfully to fulfill their charge." She is "astonished at such a hard censure," but "finding her cleare conscience a sure advocate to pleade in her case, [she] went to the prison most willingly: where with sighs and teares she past away the time till she might come to her triall." Later she learns for the first time, from Pandosto's public proclamation, that she has been accused of adultery and conspiracy. Significantly for comparison with *The Winter's Tale*, Greene gives sundry thoughts to those who throughout Bohemia hear the announcement. "This proclamation being once blazed through the countrey, although the virtuous disposition of the Queene did halfe discredit the contents, yet the sodaine and speedie passage of Egistus, and the secret departure of Franion, induced them (the circumstances throughly considered) to thinke that both the proclamation was true, and the King greatly injured: yet they pitied her case, as sorowful that so good a Ladie should be crossed with such adverse Fortune" (pp. 163-64). The accusation is indirect; Bellaria "would gladly have come to her answer, that both she might have knowne her just accusers, and cleared her selfe of that guiltless crime" (p. 164). The populace is ambivalent; only time will yield up the secret of the heroine's defamation.

Hermione is denounced by her husband in the presence of those with whom she lives. She denies Leontes' accusations, to no effect; a chorus of bystanders cries out in her behalf, to no effect. Whereas Pandosto's thinking is logical and is in fact partially corroborated by the opinions of his subjects, Leontes' "knowledge" is clearly fantastic. The formal proclamation in Greene becomes on Shakespeare's stage a series of nasty, humiliating incriminations, in language worthy of Iago. With profound irony Leontes unwittingly characterizes himself as a slanderer:

> You, my lords,
> Look on her, mark her well; be but about
> To say 'she is a goodly lady,' and
> The justice of your hearts will thereto add
> ' 'Tis pity she's not honest, honourable:'
> Praise her but for this her without-door form,
> (Which on my faith deserves high speech) and straight
> The shrug, the hum or ha, these petty brands
> That calumny doth use—O, I am out—
> That mercy does, for calumny will sear
> Virtue itself: these shrugs, these hums and ha's,
> When you have said 'she's goodly,' come between,
> Ere you can say 'she's honest:' but be't known
> From him that has most cause to grieve it should be,
> She's an adult'ress.   (II.i.64-78)

It is here that Hermione tells him, "You, my lord, / Do but mistake" (II.i.80-81). Without denigrating her accuser, she points to the villainy of slander and the sting of infamy:

> How this will grieve you,
> When you shall come to clearer knowledge, that
> You thus have publish'd me! Gentle my lord,
> You scarce can right me throughly then to say
> You did mistake.   (II.i.96-99)

She foresees that Leontes' mistake will cost him his happiness. At best she can hope now that he will sometime regain peace of mind through contrition:

> Adieu, my lord:
> I never wish'd to see you sorry; now
> I trust I shall.   (II.i.122-24)

She denies the charges, firmly and articulately. The fact that Leontes will not listen to her emphasizes the completeness of his folly. She pronounces the traditional opposition between charity and slander in requesting, "beseech you all, my lords, / With thoughts so qualified as your charities / Shall best instruct you, / measure me" (II.i.112-14). Leontes alone is uninstructed by charity. With his wife we grieve for him.

The slandered woman and her accuser in *The Winter's Tale* play their scene before spectators who report truth. Greene's guards and the Bohemian populace generally feel sympathy for Bellaria, but a lord and Antigonus, who stand for the community in Shakespeare's play, actively defend Hermione.

They form a chorus condemning the evil of the king's opinion and insisting on the value of his wife's good name not only for the royal family but for the whole society. Helplessly but insistently they try to make Leontes understand the meaning of his words. Theirs are voices of faith and truth, reminding us of what Leontes has thrown away. The lord offers to affirm Hermione's honor with his life. He is, as we know, a traditional figure; he has no name; he speaks only a few lines. His heroism is a bright flash of love. He begs the king:

> For her, my lord,
> I dare my life lay down and will do't, sir,
> Please you to accept it, that the queen is spotless
> I' the eyes of heaven and to you;—I mean,
> In this which you accuse her. (II.i.129-33)

A more realistically conceived character, whose name we know, echoes this deep anxiety. Although he speaks hyperbolically, Antigonus does not exaggerate the magnitude of the accusation or the significance of Hermione's honor.

> It is for you we speak, not for ourselves:
> You are abused, and by some putter-on
> That will be damn'd for 't; Would I knew the villain,
> I would land-damn him. Be she honour-flaw'd,
> I have three daughters. . . .
> I'll geld 'em all; fourteen they shall not see,
> To bring false generations. (II.i.140-48)

The anonymous lord's final comment points the same way:

> I had rather you did lack [credit] than I, my lord,
> Upon this ground; and more it would content me
> To have her honour true than your suspicion,
> Be blamed for't how you might. (II.i.158-61)

And Antigonus puts in a last protest, implying that the truth or falsity of Leontes' accusation is less important than the open shame of his victim: 'I wish, my liege, / You had only in your silent judgment tried it, / Without more overture" (II.i.170-72). Now Leontes announces that he has sent to Delphi for confirmation of Hermione's guilt. Shakespeare arouses our expectation that the gods will vindicate her and that Leontes' disease, although beyond the control of human beings, will be cured by the message from Apollo.

The scene in which Perdita's life is saved is an extension of this one. In the source Pandosto decides that the newborn "bastard brat" should be burned;

his nobles dissuade him from this and he commands instead that Fawnia be put to sea in a rudderless boat. The shipmen instructed to perform this task, "seeing the sweete countenance of the yong babe, began to accuse the King of rigor ... ; but feare constrayned them to that which their nature did abhorre" (p. 167). In Shakespeare, good will champions innocence and Perdita is rescued by faith. Paulina, bringing the baby to Leontes in hope that the sight of her will cure "These dangerous unsafe lunes" (II.ii.30), finds the king more certain of his error than ever. She is not afraid to call him a traitor:

> for he
> The sacred honour of himself, his queen's,
> His hopeful son's, his babe's, betrays to slander,
> Whose sting is sharper than the sword's; and will not
> For, as the case now stands, it is a curse
> He cannot be compell'd to 't—once remove
> The root of his opinion, which is rotten
> As ever oak or stone was sound.   (II.iii.82-89)

"Whose sting is sharper than the sword's": again, images of serpent and weapon coalesce. Shakespeare suggests the widening implications of Leontes' "betrayal" of himself, his wife, and his children; the stain on Hermione's reputation, however unwarranted, will affect the next generation. Paulina echoes the homilist's conception that detraction recoils upon itself:

> I'll not call you tyrant;
> But this most cruel usage of your queen,
> Not able to produce more accusation
> Than your own weak-hinged fancy, something savours
> Of tyranny and will ignoble make you,
> Yea, scandalous to the world.   (II.iii.116-21)

But Leontes' fancy cannot be shaken. Paulina prays for the baby, "Jove send her / A better guiding spirit!" (II.iii.126-27). Earlier Camillo had prayed, upon failing to uproot Leontes' suspicions, "Happy star reign now!"[3]; and the queen when denounced had reflected, "There's some ill planet reigns: / I must be patient till the heavens look / With an aspect more favourable" (II.i.105-07). These references to a transcendent force have reminded us of the helplessness of the people on the stage. Now Paulina's plan has failed. Disappointed again, we continue to wait for the messengers from Delphi. But when Leontes commands that his child be taken to the fire, Antigonus' faith in the queen interposes. Leontes asks, "What will you adventure / To save this brat's life?" The old man, on his knees with everyone else, answers:

> Any thing, my lord,
> That my ability may undergo
> And nobleness impose: at least thus much:
> I'll pawn the little blood which I have left
> To save the innocent: any thing possible.

(II.iii.162-67)

Calumny, self-destructive and inimical to life itself, is opposed by love and self-sacrifice. What is accidental in Greene, the safe landing of Fawnia's rudderless boat, becomes an act of heroism in Shakespeare. Perdita's rescue from cruelty by Paulina and Antigonus keeps our attention on the traditional ethical polarities central to the story.

So do Shakespeare's other innovations. He veers away from his source in the trial scene with its reversal; he deepens the hero's recognition; he revives the slandered heroine.

Greene's and Shakespeare's trial scenes are quite different despite conspicuous resemblances. Bellaria, "no whit dismayed" by the situation, conducts a fine defense, and the appeal to the oracle is her idea. She begs the king that for the sake of his son "he would graunt her a request, which was this, that it would please his majestie to send sixe of his noble men whome he best trusted, to the Isle of Delphos, there to enquire of the Oracle of Apollo, whether she had committed adultery with Egistus . . . " (pp. 168-69). Like Bandello's Fenicia and Boccaccio's Genevra among other non-Shakespearian heroines, this accused woman holds on spiritedly to life and hope, looking for exoneration as for the solution to a puzzle. And her plan succeeds. When later the message from the shrine comes back, Pandosto is satisfied that she is innocent. He acknowledges his mistake and begs her forgiveness. Now, pathetically, she dies; whether because of Pandosto's jealousy, or the false accusation itself, or psycho-physical stress, Greene does not decide.

While Shakespeare's borrowings from this scene in *Pandosto* are obvious and extensive, he makes honor the focal point of the dialogue and transforms Greene's heroine into a true Susanna. Hermione is an excellent witness, but Shakespeare emphasizes the futility of any defense against detraction. What Shakespeare's other slandered heroines feel, Hermione articulates. Claudio, wishing to question Hero, had asked her father to "bid her answer truly." "I charge thee do so, as thou art my child," Leonato had said; and Hero, feeling the irony of the situation, had cried, "O, God defend me! how am I beset!" (IV.i.76-80). Shakespeare's last slandered heroine explains:

> Since what I am to say must be but that
> Which contradicts my accusation and

87

> The testimony on my part no other
> But what comes from myself, it shall scarce boot me
> To say 'not guilty:' mine integrity
> Being counted falsehood, shall, as I express it,
> Be so received. (III.ii.23-39)

Once again, Shakespeare accentuates the worthlessness of a life stained by slander. Threatened with death, Hermione says:

> To me can life be no commodity:
> The crown and comfort of my life, your favour,
> I do give lost; for I do feel it gone,
> But know not how it went. (III.ii.94-97)

Prizing life "not a straw," the queen speaks only to shield her reputation: "for honour, / 'Tis a derivative from me to mine, / And only that I stand for" (III.ii.44-46). And she upholds Leontes' honor even while he is doing his utmost to undermine it. Maintaining a tone of respect and sympathy for this benighted man (unlike anything in Greene), she wishes that the scene of her misery be looked on "with eyes / Of pity, not revenge" (III.ii.123-24).

Shakespeare invents a new climax for the borrowed story. In doing so he dramatizes the tremendous power of false opinion and the deadliness of misguided speech. Hermione's testimony is predictably ineffectual, and she refers her case to the oracle. But whereas Greene's slander plot here reaches its turning point, Shakespeare violates our expectation that now Leontes will come to his senses. Pandosto immediately accepts Apollo's verdict, but Leontes blasphemes, shockingly, "There is no truth at all i' the oracle" (III.ii.141). In bringing his hero to the conclusion that the gods themselves are liars, Shakespeare points—more clearly than ever before—to the ultimate meaning of slander. Stunned, we wonder if anything can dissipate this man's dream. Then it is suddenly exploded by the news of his son's death. Leontes immediately sees this as a judgment: "Apollo's angry; and the heavens themselves / Do strike at my injustice" (III.ii.147-48). His sudden reversal reminds us of Posthumus'; in assuming that heaven is punishing him for impiety he resembles the hero of the *Miracle d'Oton*. By changing the turning point from the gods' decree to the boy's death, Shakespeare emphasizes the human cost of Leontes' sin. Now undeceived, the hero begins to understand it. He looks at the wreckage of his mistake: the betrayed friend, the dishonored servant, the dead children. And now, Paulina tells him,

> the queen, the queen,
> The sweet'st, dear'st creature's dead, and vengeance for't
> Not dropp'd down yet. (III.ii.202-03)

Leontes' recognition is much deeper than Pandosto's. It begins here as he listens to Paulina speak about the magnitude of his responsibility:

> Do not repent these things, for they are heavier
> Than all thy woes can stir: therefore betake thee
> To nothing but despair.   A thousand knees
> Ten thousand years together, naked, fasting,
> Upon a barren mountain, and still winter
> In storm perpetual, could not move the gods
> To look that way thou wert.   (III.ii.209-14)

Her hyperbole suggests eternal damnation, recalling the old association of Leontes' sin with the fallen angel. The slanderer can finally hear the words of True Report. He accepts her judgment:

> Prithee, bring me
> To the dead bodies of my queen and son:
> One grave shall be for both: upon them shall
> The causes of their death appear, unto.
> Our shame perpetual.   (III.ii.235-39)

This hero's contrition is analogous to Claudio's formal rite at Hero's grave, to Othello's last speech, to Posthumus' soliloquy of penitence. He dedicates himself to a lifetime of repentance:

> Once a day I'll visit
> The chapel where they lie, and tears shed there
> Shall be my recreation: so long as nature
> Will bear up with this exercise, so long
> I daily vow to use it.   Come, and lead me
> Unto these sorrows.   (III.ii.239-44)

Repentance is thematic in Shakespeare, not in Greene. For sixteen years (Time tells us) Leontes grieves, understanding that he had, in taking integrity for falsehood, destroyed his world single-handedly. His sense of the enormity of his mistake now matches Camillo's and Paulina's. Finally his friends think his suffering should end. One of them says:

> Sir, you have done enough, and have perform'd
> A saint-like sorrow: no fault could you make,
> Which you have not redeem'd; indeed, paid down
> More penitence than done trespass: at the last,
> Do as the heavens have done, forget your evil;
> With them forgive yourself.   (V.i.1-6)

But Leontes still thinks of the irreversible damage: "The wrong I did myself; which was so much, / That heirless it hath made my kingdom and / Destroy'd the sweet'st companion that e'er man / Bred his hopes out of" (V.i.9-12).

So Leontes atones—and Hermione comes back to life. Or at least the illusion that his contrition and regained faith revive her, leaves an impression more lasting than the naturalistic explanation which she gives. The preservation of this slandered heroine's life is, of course, Shakespeare's most radical innovation. But his management of it is thoroughly traditional, for again, the restorative power is True Report's and the ending is a miracle. That Leontes' contrition is necessary for the happy ending but not enough in itself is suggested by the role of Paulina (wholly Shakespeare's creation) in Act Five. She who had instantly perceived that Leontes' accusation was false and had argued with him, who had later shown him the meaning of his error and taught him contrition, now takes charge of his future. She instructs him in the gods' secret purposes. When Dion expresses the wish that the king remarry "for present comfort and for future good," Paulina recalls the oracle expressing the gods' will:

> . . . has not the divine Apollo said,
> Is 't not the tenour of his oracle,
> That King Leontes shall not have an heir
> Till his lost child be found?   which that it shall,
> Is all as monstrous to our human reason
> As my Antigonus to break his grave
> And come again to me; who, on my life,
> Did perish with the infant.   'Tis your counsel
> My lord should to the heavens be contrary,
> Oppose against their wills.   [*To Leontes.*]
>   Care not for issue;
> The crown will find an heir.   (V.i.37-47)

We know that Perdita lives, but Paulina does not; as we watch, we are caught by what seems a pure faith; our hope mounts.[4] Leontes must trust her. And he does, putting his life in her hands: "My true Paulina, / We shall not marry till thou bid'st us." She hints faintly at the ending when she answers, "That / Shall be when your first queen's again in breath; / Never till then" (V.i.81-84). John Lawlor says about the way in which Shakespeare manages Perdita's preservation, "We have moved away from the conscious purposes and dilemmas of Greene's story to awareness of a destiny which will bring the persons of the play to ends they cannot foresee."[5] This is true especially of Hermione's revival, an ending foreseen by no one except Paulina.

For although Hermione gives Perdita a realistic explanation for her resurrection (". . . I, / Knowing by Paulina that the oracle / Gave hope thou wast in being, have preserved / Myself to see the issue" [V.iii.125-28]), what we witness is a miracle. The worker of it tells the observers, "It is required / You do awake your faith" (V.iii.94-95). Leontes, having sorrowed for sixteen years, has regained faith. We all watch the statue; Paulina proceeds:

> Music, awake her; strike!
> 'Tis time; descend; be stone no more; approach;
> Strike all that look upon with marvel.   Come,
> I'll fill your grave up: stir, nay, come away,
> Bequeath to death your numbness, for from him
> Dear life redeems you.   (V.iii.98-103)

And the statue stirs. Another Susanna is reclaimed. In a deeper way than in Greene's story the happy ending is a "triumph of time," the result of Leontes' long expiation for his mistake. In *The Winter's Tale* Shakespeare reduces to its essence the inveterate opposition between slander and love, dramatizing more plainly and audaciously than ever before the deep evil of Ill Report. Leontes in deed has resembled Shakespeare's "most replenish'd villain" (II.i.79), although his intentions have been the opposite. The element of deliberate wickedness is gone, and only misguided speech remains; but this, we now see, is equally injurious—or nearly so. For despite the happy ending, our sense of loss is tremendous.[6] Shakespeare's inquiry into slander closes with this play,[7] for he has finally imagined "the injury of tongues," the thing itself.

NOTES

NOTES TO CHAPTER ONE

1 *Richard II*, I.i.171 (*The Complete Works of Shakespeare*, ed. Hardin Craig [Glenview, Ill., 1961]). All my Shakespeare quotations are from this edition.

2 *Richard II*, I.i.177-83.

3 *Cymbeline*, III.iv.36.

4 Morton Bloomfield, *The Seven Deadly Sins* (East Lansing, 1952). Rosamond Tuve studies aspects of the development of the Sins tradition in two articles, "Notes on the Virtues and Vices," *JWCI*, XXVI (1963), 264-303, and XXVII (1964), 42-72, and in *Allegorical Imagery* (Princeton, 1966). Siegfried Wenzel's "The Seven Deadly Sins: Some Problems of Research," *Speculum*, XLIII (1968), 1-22 discusses recent scholarship on the Sins.

5 *Jacob's Well*, ed. Arthur Brandeis (EETS, O.S., No. 115 [London, 1900]), p. 82. Throughout this study, the sense of the English word "envy" intended is that of the first OED definition: "malignant or hostile feeling; ill will; malice, enmity."

6 *Rhetorica* (*The Works of Aristotle*, tr. Rhys Roberts [Oxford, 1946], Vol. XI), II.x.1387b.

7 Tr. Frank J. Miller (Loeb ed., 1925), 768-82.

8 Lucretius' lines become very famous; he writes of those who "waste with envy" because another is powerful, regarded, and "walks clothed with bright renown; while they complain that they themselves are wrapped in darkness and the mire"—*De Rerum Natura*, tr. Cyril Bailey (Oxford, 1949), Vol. I, III.75-77; also Horace's "The envious man grows lean when his neighbour waxes fat; than envy Sicilian tyrants invented no worse torture" (*Satires, Epistles and Ars Poetica*, tr. H. Rushton Fairclough [Loeb ed., 1932], *Epistles*, I.ii.57-59).

9 *Culex* (*Virgil*, tr. H. Rushton Fairclough [Loeb ed., 1954], Vol. II), 341-42.

10 *Satires*, II.i.76-78.

11 "Of Envy and Hate" (*Moralia*, tr. Phillip De Lacy [Loeb ed., 1959], Vol. VII), 537 F.

12 *Tristia* (*Ovid: Tristia, Ex Ponto*, tr. Arthur Leslie Wheeler [Loeb ed., 1924]), IV.x.121-24.

[13] *Pro Balbo* (*The Speeches of Cicero*, tr. R. Gardner [Loeb ed., 1958], Vol. II), XXVI.57-58.

[14] *Satires*, I.iii.60-61.

[15] *The Eunuch* (*Terence*, tr. John Sargeaunt [Loeb ed., 1912], Vol. 1), 411-412.

[16] *Ovid's Fasti*, tr. Sir James George Frazer (Loeb ed., 1931), I. 74.

[17] Wisdom of Solomon 2:23-24 (*Vulgate*).

[18] Saint Basil, *Concerning Envy* (*Writings of Saint Basil*, tr. Sister Monica Wagner [New York, 1950], Vol. I), p. 465.

[19] Saint Cyprian, *Jealousy and Envy* (*Treatises*, tr. Roy J. Deferrari [New York, 1958]), p. 302. I have also consulted the Migne reprint of the original.

[20] *Cf*. Plutarch, "On Envy and Hate," 537E: "But men deny that they envy . . . ; and if you show that they do, they allege any number of excuses and say that they are angry with the fellow or fear or hate him, cloaking and concealing their envy with whatever other name occurs to them for their passion, implying that among the disorders of the soul it is alone unmentionable."

[21] Romans 3:13-14. *V*. also Psalm 10:7 ("His mouth is full of cursing and deceit and fraud: under his tongue is mischief and vanity").

[22] *The Book of Vices and Virtues*, ed. W. Nelson Francis (EETS, O.S., No. 217 [London, 1942]), p. 23.

[23] "Good Name in *Othello*," *SEL*, VII (1967), 202, n. 19; 202.

[24] *Mirour de l'Omme* (*The Complete Works of John Gower*, ed. G. C. Macaulay, Vol. I [1899]), 7393.

[25] *Confessio Amantis* (*The Complete Works of John Gower*, ed. G. C. Macaulay, Vol. II [1901]), II.3130.

[26] Revelation 12:10.

[27] Ecclesiastes 7:1 ("A good name is better than precious ointment").

[28] Proverbs 25:18 ("A man that beareth false witness against his neighbour is a maul, a sword, and a sharp arrow").

[29] Frederick Padelford, ed. Spenser, *The Faerie Queene*, I (Baltimore, 1932), 414.

[30] Lydgate, *The Pilgrimage of the Life of Man* (EETS, No. 306 [1904]), 14893-907.

[31] This kind of metaphor reminds us of the traditional classification of detraction among the Sins of the Mouth (Gluttony).

[32] *Golden Epistles*, 1595, K_2.

[33] William Baldwin, *A Treatise of Morall Philosophie*, ed. Robin H. Bowers (Gainesville, 1967), p. 321.

[34] *The English Works of Sir Thomas More*, ed. W. E. Campbell (London, 1931), Vol. I, 481.

[35] *An Exposition upon Nehemiah* (*The Works of James Pilkington*, ed. James Scholefield [Cambridge, 1842]), pp. 336-37.

[36] Geoffrey Whitney, *A Choice of Emblemes* (Leyden, 1586), p. 24.

[37] "The Reading of an Elizabethan: Some Sources of the Prose Pamphlets of Thomas Lodge," *RES*, VIII (1932), 277.

[38] "Notes on the Virtues and Vices," *JWCI*, XXVII (1964), 48, n. 78.

[39] Thomas Lodge, *Wits Miserie and the Worlds Madnesse: Discouering the Deuils Incarnat of this Age*, 1596 (*Complete Works*, Hunterian Club [1883], Vol. IV), p. 55.

[40] *The Countesse of Pembrokes Arcadia* (*The Prose Works of Sir Phillip Sidney*, ed. Albert Feuillerat [Cambridge, 1963], Vol. I), p. 203.

[41] *The Plays of George Chapman*, ed. Thomas M. Parrott (New York, 1961), Vol. I, II.i.5-18.

[42] *The Peacemaker* (*The Works of Thomas Middleton*, ed. A. H. Bullen [New York, 1964], Vol. VIII), p. 333. Madeleine Doran in "Good Name in *Othello*" cites other Renaissance characterizations, literary and graphic (p. 202, notes 17, 18; p. 203, n. 22; p, 206, n. 28). There are many citations in Samuel Chew, *The Virtues Reconciled* (Toronto, 1947), and *The Pilgrimage of Life* (New Haven, 1962). Traditional descriptions of Envy are legion in Shakespeare's century. See also Thomas Tusser, *Fiue Hundred Pointes of Good Husbandrie*, 1557 (London, 1878), pp. 146-47; Barnaby Googe, *Eclogs, Epitaphes, and Sonettes*, 1563 (Gainesville, 1968), pp. 4-7; Stephen Bateman, *A christall glasse of christian reformation*, 1569, G_3 ff.; Anthony Munday, *The Mirror of Mutabilitie*, A_4 ff.; Nicholas Breton, *The Pilgrimage to Paradise*, 1592, C_2, E_3 ff.; Francis Sabie, *Adams Complaint*, 1596, C_4v; John Lane, *Tom Tel-Troths Message*, 1600 (London, 1948), pp. 123 ff.; John Norden, *The labyrinth of mans life*, 1614, H_1; John Earle, "A Detractor" (*Micro-Cosmographie* [Cambridge, 1903]), pp. 67-69; John Day, *Peregrinatio Scholastica*, 1625 (*The Works of John Day*, ed. A. H. Bullen [London, 1881], Vol. II), pp. 56-57; Phineas Fletcher, *The Purple Island*, c. 1611-27 (Giles and Phineas Fletcher, *Poetical Works*, ed. Frederick Boas [Cambridge, 1909], Vol. II), pp. 95 ff.

[43] *Virgidemiae*, 1598 (*The Collected Poems of Joseph Hall*, ed. A. Davenport [Liverpool, 1949]), "His Defiance to Enuie," 23.

[44] *Matilda the faire* (*The Works of Michael Drayton*, ed. J. William Hebel [Oxford, 1961], Vol. I), p. 228.

[45] Peter Pett, *Times Journey to seeke his Daughter Truth; and Truths Letter to Fame of Englands Excellencie* (1599), Dv.

[46] "Of Honor and Reputation" (*The Essays of Francis Bacon*, ed. Clark Sutherland Northrup [Boston, 1908]), p. 164.

47 "Tempora Mutantur, et Nos Mutamur in Illis," from *Penelope's Web* (*The Plays and Poems of Robert Greene*, ed. J. Churton Collins [Freeport, New York, 1970], Vol. II), p. 240.

48 John Marston, *The Scourge of Villanie* (1599), ed. G. B. Harrison (New York, 1925), p. 1.

49 Pett, D_2.

50 Baldwin, p. 322.

51 *The Catechism of Thomas Becon*, ed. John Ayre (Cambridge, 1844), pp. 116-19.

52 *The Poetical Works of Edmund Spenser*, ed. J. C. Smith and E. de Selincourt (London, 1961), I.ii.9.

53 Spenser, *The Faerie Queene*, ed. Frederick Padelford, II (Baltimore, 1932), 227.

54 Edwin Greenlaw, "A Better Teacher than Aquinas," *SP*, XIV (1917), 204.

55 Quoted in Charles G. Smith, "Spenser's Theory of Friendship: An Elizabethan Commonplace," *SP*, XXXII (1935), 162.

56 Smith, p. 158.

57 H. S. V. Jones, *A Spenser Handbook* (New York, 1930), p. 239.

58 A. C. Judson, "Spenser's Theory of Courtesy," *PMLA*, XLVII (1932), 130-31.

59 Judson, p. 131.

60 *Hamlet*, I.iii.38.

61 Spenser defines Occasion in Book Two, in which Guyon succeeds in putting an iron lock on Occasion's "vngratious tong" (II.iv.12); McManaway showed that Spenser's "unclassical figure of Occasion" is partly indebted to figures of Discord and Envy in the emblem books (James McManaway, "'Occasion,' *Faerie Queene* II. 4-5," *MLN*, XLIX [1934], 391-93). Certainly "Occasion, the root of all wrath and despight" (II.iv.10) is connected in Spenser's mind not only with her actual son Furor, but also with Envy and thus with the Beast.

62 *The Allegory of Love* (Oxford, 1936), p. 350.

63 Judson, pp. 134, 132.

NOTES TO CHAPTER TWO

1 Ariosto and Bandello are translated in Geoffrey Bullough, *Narrative and Dramatic Sources of Shakespeare*, II (New York, 1958); Beverley's *Ariodanto and Jenevra* is reprinted in Charles T. Prouty's *The Sources of Much Ado about Nothing* (New Haven, 1950); *The Rocke of Regard* was reprinted by J. P. Collier (London, 1866-70).

² Spenser's story of Phedon in Book II of *The Faerie Queene*, an important analogue, is also a departure from the "realistic" sources.

³ *Commody of the moste vertuous and Godlye Susanna*, ed. B. Ifor Evans and W. W. Greg (Oxford, 1937).

⁴ This durable type-story is very widespread in medieval and Renaissance literature. Paul Christopherson (in *The Ballad of Sir Aldingar* [Oxford, 1952], pp. 114-15) emphasizes the importance of the story of Susanna as an old and popular form of the slandered woman tale. Baron Rothschild lists dramas on Susanna in ten languages; most of them date from the sixteenth century. There was a *sacra rappresentazione*, now lost, of about 1500 (*Le Mistere du Viel Testament*, V [1885], lxvi-cxi). Craig demonstrated that this was an important dramatic subject in sixteenth-century Biblical drama (*English Drama of the Middle Ages* [Oxford, 1955], p. 364). Marvin Herrick discusses the sixteenth-century Susanna play ("Susanna and the Elders in Sixteenth-Century Drama," *Studies in Honor of T. W. Baldwin*, ed. Don Cameron Allen [Urbana, 1958], pp. 125-35), attributing the perennial popularity of the tale among dramatists to the fact that "it is an excellent story in the original biblical version, inherently dramatic rather than narrative" (p. 126). Greene based two novels on the subject (*Works*, ed. A. B. Grosart [London, 1881-86]), "Mirrour of Modestie" (III) and "Francescoes Fortunes" (VII). We may remember that Sir Toby Belch quotes the first line of a broadside ballad entitled "The Constancy of Susanna" and also that Shakespeare's daughter was named Susanna.

⁵ *Endeavors of Art* (Madison, 1954), p. 188.

⁶ In Prouty, p. 97.

⁷ By this I do not mean to reduce Don John, who is a believable human being in the play, to an allegorical silhouette. But the elements of the characterization and the remarks he makes all fit together into the personality pattern recognized by the allegorical writers. In two of the analogues of *Much Ado* there are characters whose similarity to Don John has been noticed. In Bandello the rival for the heroine's love gets help from a man "apt to serve his blind and frenzied appetite," "a young courtier, a fellow of little upbringing, more pleased with evil than with good" (in Bullough, p. 115). Belleforest's tale contains a similar servant. These characters may have suggested Don John to Shakespeare, but he changed the story a great deal by making the man of simple malice the prime mover in the plot against Hero.

⁸ *Shakespeare and the Allegory of Evil* (New York, 1958), p. 411. Spivack showed what both Don John and Iago owe to the Vice tradition, and he also suggested links between the Vice figure and the Seven Deadly Sins.

⁹ This exclamation is reminiscent of Lydgate's Detraction, boasting of her status as Envy's cook (15444). Don John speaks of "food to my displeasure" (I.iii.66) as Gower had written about the slanderer feeding on the ills of others (*Mirour*, 2749-60).

[10] *Mirour de l'Omme* (*The Complete Works of John Gower*, ed. G. C. Macaulay, Vol. I [1901]), 2730.

[11] This is even clearer because Shakespeare also uses paid slanderers in the play. Traditionally avarice as well as envy has been regarded as a motivation for the detractor: *Jacob's Well* numbers among the accursed all those "that for malyce, or wynnyng, or fauour, or for ony other cause, dyffamyn or slaunderyn ony persone, and apeyryn his name among gode men and worschipfull..." (ed. Arthur Brandeis, EETS, O. S., No. 115 [London, 1900], p. 150). In *The Spanish Tragedie* the victim of slander speaks to his accuser: "My guiltles death will be aueng'd on thee, / On thee, Villuppo, that hath malisde thus, / Or for thy meed hast falsely me accusde" (*The Works of Thomas Kyd*, ed. Frederick S. Boas [Oxford, 1901], III.i.51-53. In *Much Ado*, the motive of the malicious, "rich" villain is distinguished from that of the "poor" accomplice whom he hires (III.iii.118-20). Don John is "the devil my master" to Borachio (III.iii. 164), who belies Hero for a thousand ducats.

[12] P. 76.

[13] In Bullough, p. 95.

[14] P. 76.

[15] This may be the reason for Shakespeare's carelessness about Margaret's role in the plot against Hero. As we hear about the window-scene, all our attention is attracted, not to the practicalities of the stratagem at all, but to the fact that an outrageous falsehood has been circulated.

[16] Madeleine Doran (*Endeavors of Art*, p. 179) has pointed out the parallel between the denunciation scene in *Much Ado* and the one in Della Porta's *Gli Duoi Fratelli Rivali*. Although in the Italian play the scene does not take place onstage, the account of it contains these resemblances to the one in *Much Ado*: the hero makes his accusation on the wedding day; the heroine's father immediately denounces her, with great anger; at this point she faints and apparently dies. Della Porta places much stress on themes of honor, fame, and infamy. The report of the denunciation scene in his play brings out the maliciousness of slander, as the Shakespearian scene does, by emphasizing the girl's helplessness and her father's harshness.

[17] In Bullough, p. 118.

[18] P. 28.

[19] The Renaissance debate about the value of reputation, and the vast discussion of honor of which it was a part, are not substantially relevant to Shakespeare's plays on the slandered woman. It is a commonplace proposition in the sixteenth century that honor only fortuitously reflects virtue. As Montaigne puts it in "Of Glorie," "I care not so much what I am with others, as I respect what I am in my selfe" (*Essayes*, tr. John Florio, ed. Desmond MacCarthy, Vol. II [London, 1928], 348; Du Vair writes, "The things which are out of our power are these; our riches, reputation, and briefly, that which doth no way depend of our willes" (Guillaume Du

Vair, *The Moral Philosophie of the Stoicks*, ed. Rudolph Kirk [New Brunswick, 1951], p. 68). Iago's criticisms of reputation are widely prevalent. But Shakespeare assumes the other, the traditional view in these plays. Honor for his slandered heroines and their friends and families is "a certeine testemonie of vertue shining of yt self, geven of some man by the judgement of good men" (Robert Ashley, *Of Honour*, ed. Virgil B. Heltzel [San Marino, 1947], p. 34). See Madeleine Doran's analysis of the interpretation of *infamia* inherited from Roman law ("Good Name in *Othello*, *SEL*, VII [1967], 196-98). D. J. Gordon in "Name and Fame: Shakespeare's *Coriolanus*" (*Papers Mainly Shakespearian*, ed. George Duthie [Edinburgh, 1964], pp. 40-57) shows that in *Coriolanus* Shakespeare is working within a scheme constituted by the words *fama, laus, existimatio, opinio, vox, honor, nomen*, "a set of words describing certain relationships between a man and other men, all seen as together forming a group or community" (p. 46). Words "are what the community says about [a man]. They must be right, and the rightness of the relationship lies in its truth. It must be true between speaker and word, and true between word and thing. Language, what people say to each other about things, is constitutive of society, of the civil life" (p. 49). Although obviously Shakespeare is familiar with the other view, this is the sense that governs his stories of Hero, Desdemona, Imogen, and Hermione.

[20] In Prouty, p. 129.

[21] The French *Miracle d'Oton, roi d'espagne* and *Miracle de la Marquise de la Gaudine* (in *Miracles de Nostre Dame*, ed. G. Paris and U. Robert [Paris, 1876-93]) and Italian *Santa Uliva, Santa Guglielma*, and *Stella* (in *Sacre Rappresentazioni dei Secoli XIV, XV e XVI*, ed. A. D'Ancona [Florence, 1872]) all belong to different cycles or subgroups of the type-story of the slandered and exculpated heroine, but they resemble one another and the Susanna story formally. The heroines have different kinds of persecutors and undergo various kinds of sufferings; but in each case a miracle like the one that saves Susanna rescues them from sufferings caused by another's "invidia," "malizia," "envie," or "haine." It is noteworthy that they compare themselves, in distress or thankfulness, to Susanna. Having been approached by her would-be seducer, Guglielma soliloquizes: "O Dio, tu sia mia scorta e mia defesa; Susanna so che fu per te salvata" (*Sacra Rappresentazioni*, III, 216). Nostre Dame says of the Marquise de la Gaudine, " ... elle est une Susanne voir / Accusée de grief meffait, / Lequel elle n'a pas meffait" (*Miracles*, II, 1072-74).

[22] The theme is conventional. The prayer of Chaucer's Constance to "Immortal God, that savedst Susanne / Fro false blame" is answered by a hand that smites her calumniator and a marvellous voice pronouncing her innocence (*The Man of Law's Tale*, in *The Works of Geoffrey Chaucer*, ed. F. N. Robinson [Cambridge, Mass., 1933], 639 ff.). In Elyot's description of the "Calumny" of Appelles the victim of Detraction is holding his hands toward heaven, "calling God and the saints for witness" (Sir Thomas Elyot, *The Book named the Governor* [Everyman ed., 1962], p. 235); see also Baldwin, p. 26 above.

[23] I have not used Whetstone's version in my comparisons, because his story leaves out the slander theme entirely. There is no accusation of unchastity.

[24] Whether or not Shakespeare actually knew Garter's play is not important; the continuity between the drama of his time and the type of drama which lies behind *Susanna* has been demonstrated. Manly showed "that the miracle play did not differ in any essential from the romantic comedy and tragedy [of the period immediately preceding the advent of Marlowe and Shakespeare] and consequently that it was probably in the miracle play, rather than in the better-known Scripture play and morality, that the techniques of the stage of Shakespeare were developed." One cannot draw a line in medieval literature between "saints' legends and romance: the incidents are the same; the material is identical" (John M. Manly, "The Miracle Play in England," *RSL*, ser. 3, VII [1927], 153).

NOTES TO CHAPTER THREE

[1] Geoffrey Bullough, *Narrative and Dramatic Sources of Shakespeare*, VII (New York, 1973), 244.

[2] See p. 14, above.

[3] *Mirour de l'Omme (The Complete Works of John Gower*, ed. G. C. Macaulay, Vol. I [1899]), 3766-68.

[4] In *"Lost" Tudor Plays*, ed. John S. Farmer (New York, 1966), p. 117.

[5] For a review see Robert Heilman's notes to his chapter on Iago in *Magic in the Web* (Lexington, 1956). Also *v.* Helen Gardner, "The Noble Moor," *Proc. Brit. Acad.*, XLI (1955), 189-205; Bernard Spivack, *Shakespeare and the Allegory of Evil* (New York, 1958); Leah Scragg, "Iago—Vice or Devil," *Shakespeare Survey*, XXI (1968), 53-65; Madeleine Doran, "Good Name in *Othello*," *SEL*, VII (1967), 195-217; Helen Gardner, "*Othello*: A Retrospect, 1900-67," *Shakespeare Survey*, XXI (1968), 1-11. Bullough concludes, "Iago is neither Vice nor Devil, though he combines both traditions" (p. 232). A Ph.D. dissertation by Myra Brenner (Brandeis, 1970), *Shakespeare and Elizabethan Concepts of Envy*, contains much background material, separated into the "humanist" and the "penitential" traditions; her application of this material to various Shakespearian characters, including Iago, differs from mine in kind and in purpose.

[6] P. 18.

[7] E. E. Stoll, *Shakespeare and Other Masters* (Cambridge, Mass., 1940), p. 252.

[8] Helen Gardner, "The Noble Moor," p. 197.

[9] In characterizing False Seeming Gower, alluding to Habakkuk 2:15, writes of the man who gives his friend a drink "mingled with gall" and then publicizes his drunkenness, so that his glory is destroyed, he is "despoiled and scorned" (*Mirour*, 3602-09).

[10] See above, p. 15.

[11] All Iago's victims possess in large measure the virtues traditionally opposed to Envy's sub-sins. Praise is the opposite of Detraction; *v.* Cassio's speeches in II.i especially. "Conjoie" and Compassion are the feelings antithetical to envious grief and joy; "Conjoie" delights in others' good fortune, beauty, etc. (Cassio: "My hopes do shape him for the governor" [II.i.54]). Good Intention (saying plainly what is meant and nothing more) is the reverse of False Seeming. Support will suffer for the benefit of others. Iago counts on, manipulates, all these traits in the protagonists, all manifestations of their charity.

[12] "Good Name in *Othello*," pp. 208-09.

[13] *Jealousy and Envy* (*Treatises*, tr. Roy J. Deferrari [New York, 1958]), pp. 297-98.

[14] P. 224.

[15] Supplanting veers toward, can appear to proceed from, Pride. Gower's Confessor, in the link between his two stories illustrating Supplanting, deplores what happens "whan Pride is with Envie joint" (II.2791). *Cf.* Lodge's Worldly Fear, the third son of his Envy, and this from Mowbray's confession in the *Mirror for Magistrates*:

> . . . see howe pride and envy joyntly runne,
> Because my prince dyd more than me, preferre
> Syr Henry Bolenbroke
> . . .
>
> Proude I that would alone be blasyng sterre,
> Envyed this Earle, for nought saue that the shine,
> Of his desertes dyd glyster more then mine.

(*The Mirror for Magistrates*, ed. Lily B. Campbell [Cambridge, 1938], p. 104)

[16] P. 16.

[17] P. 13.

[18] Helen Gardner, "*Othello*: A Retrospect, 1900-67," p. 4, referring to statements of this view by John Bayley (*The Characters of Love*) and John Holloway (*The Story of the Night*).

NOTES TO CHAPTER FOUR

[1] Edwin A. Greenlaw, "The Vows of Baldwin," *PMLA*, XXI (1906), 625. Gaston Paris discussed the wager story in *La Littérature française au moyen âge* (Paris, 1888), p. 83, and "Le Cycle de la 'Gageure,' " *Romania*, XXXII (1906), 481-551.

[2] In Geoffrey Bullough, *Narrative and Dramatic Sources of Shakespeare*, VIII (London, 1975), 51.

[3] In Bullough, p. 63.

4 J. M. Nosworthy, New Arden *Cymbeline* (London, 1955), p. xix; Bullough, p. 16. *Frederyke of Jennen*, translated from a fifteenth-century German story, was printed in English three times between 1518 and 1560 (William Flint Thrall, "*Cymbeline*, Boccaccio and the Wager Story in England," *SP*, XXVIII [1931], 639-51). A story in *Westward for Smelts* (reprinted in the Variorum *Cymbeline*) has been regarded as a source for Shakespeare's wager play, but the book was probably not published until 1620 (Bullough, p. 16, n. 1).

5 *Miracles de Nostre Dame*, ed. Gaston Paris and Ulysse Robert, IV (Paris, 1879).

6 Thrall lists a number of non-Boccaccian resemblances between *Cymbeline* and the *Miracle*. Many are similarities in detail; those corresponding to the features here discussed are: "villain alleges husband's infidelity in Rome in urging his own suit; ladies repulse villains in similar words; . . . heroes rebuked in visions for their incredulity" (p. 649, n. 43).

7 The two settings correspond to a stage in the history of the slandered woman story as recounted by Margaret Schlauch (*Chaucer's Constance and Accused Queens* [New York, 1927]). In folk tales the heroine is accused typically by demons, witches, mothers-in-law, or step-mothers. These primitive persecutors are later replaced by a villain whose motive is either ambition or rejected love. The transition is illustrated frequently in medieval literature; Chaucer's *Constance* blends primitive features with more sophisticated ones (p. 113).

8 In Bullough, p. 54.

9 In Bullough, p. 65.

10 P. 608.

11 In Bullough, p. 54.

12 In Bullough, p. 66.

13 Variorum *Cymbeline*, pp. 474, 476.

14 Two Old French romances, the *Roman de la Violette* and the *Roman du Compte de Poitiers*, also present the villain's serious attempt on the woman's honor. It is thought that the Italian type of the wager plot is derivative from the Old French type; the confrontation between the villain and heroine therefore may be considered as one of the features which the Italian tradition minimized.

15 In Bullough, pp. 56-57.

16 In Bullough, p. 71.

17 Posthumus' reaction to the false accusation has been much criticized. His credulity and rage, and his violent denunciation of all women, set him apart from the more sympathetic heroes in the *Decameron* and *Frederyke*, who are hurt and woeful; but Posthumus' behavior is conventional. The husband in the miracle play is angry and vengeful also. The comparison is

reminiscent of that between Claudio and his counterparts. Homer Swander (in "*Cymbeline* and the 'Blameless Hero,' " *ELH* [1964], 259-70), however, thinks that Shakespeare took the source material in the opposite direction; that he intended to portray Posthumus as an inadequate hero, one who progresses "toward an excellence defined largely by a rejection of conventional values" (p. 260).

[18] In Bullough, p. 59.

[19] Ohle, referred to in Paris, p. 514, n. 4.

[20] In Bullough, p. 71.

[21] New Arden *Cymbeline*, p. 152, n.

[22] The story in *Westward for Smelts*, even if later than *Cymbeline*, reinforces the contrast between Shakespeare's wager play and its close analogues. Here too the villain, recognizing the heroine's modesty, quickly gives up any idea of attempting seduction; the woman and the servant are both unaware that she has been falsely accused; the heroine, although extremely distressed (like Imogen), cleverly extricates herself from her difficulties.

[23] Nosworthy calls attention to the use of Jupiter as one of several important resemblances between *Cymbeline* and *The Rare Triumphes of Love and Fortune* (1589); the influence of this play on Shakespeare, he thinks, has been underestimated (New Arden *Cymbeline*, xxv-xxvi). Bullough also discusses the element of divine supervision in the two dramas.

[24] Hallet Smith (*Shakespeare's Romances* [San Marino, 1972], pp. 211-213) briefly reviews criticism of *Cymbeline* as a mixture of two different kinds of materials, the wager story and the historical element.

[25] W. W. Lawrence, on the other hand, felt that what interested Shakespeare most "was the earlier part of the tale," rather than Posthumus' plan to punish Imogen and the final reconciliation (*Shakespeare's Problem Comedies* [New York, 1931], p. 195).

NOTES TO CHAPTER FIVE

[1] In Geoffrey Bullough, *Narrative and Dramatic Sources of Shakespeare*, VIII (London, 1975), 165. Further references to *Pandosto* are in my text.

[2] Robert Ashley, *Of Honour*, ed. Virgil B. Heltzel (San Marino, 1947), p. 34.

[3] I.ii.363.

[4] That it is not, in fact, a pure faith (since Paulina knows that Hermione is alive) makes no difference dramatically. The audience knows only about the heir of whose loss she seems so certain.

[5] "*Pandosto* and the Nature of Dramatic Romance," *PQ*, XLI (1962), 108.

[6] For Clifford Leech it is total: only *The Winter's Tale* among Shakespeare's last plays, he writes, "faces the realization that repentance is not

enough, that 'reunion' is a bogus word, that the only finality (within the world around us) is loss" ("The Structure of the Last Plays," *Shakespeare Survey*, 11 [1958], 30).

7 The concordance reveals dozens of lines scattered throughout Shakespeare on envy, malice, slander, calumny, detraction, name, fame, and other components of the tradition, as well as many conventional images and other linguistic echoes. These further suggest his consciousness of, and interest in, the theme we have examined.

www.ingramcontent.com/pod-product-compliance
Lightning Source LLC
Chambersburg PA
CBHW050947030426
42339CB00007B/331